DR. C

The Cure *is in the* Forest

The healing powers
of wild chaga mushroom,
birch bark, and poplar buds
—the forest's most powerful
natural medicines.

KNOWLEDGE
HOUSE
PUBLISHERS

Printed in the United States of America

ISBN: 978-1-931078-33-7

Disclaimer: This book is not intended as a substitute for medical diagnosis or treatment. Anyone who has a serious disease should consult a physician before initiating any change in treatment or before beginning any new treatment.

To order this or additional Knowledge House books call: 1-866-626-5888 or order via the web at: www.knowledgehousepublishers.com

To get an order form send a SASE to:
Knowledge House Publishers
105 East Townline Rd., Unit 116
Vernon Hills, IL 60061

The
Cure
is in the
Forest

Table of Contents

Introduction

The forests are teeming with cures for all that ails the human race. Commonly, trees are regarded as beneficial for their fuel and structural components. Yet, perhaps even more important are the natural medicines which are found in trees. In fact, in these vigorous plants the most powerful of all cures are found.

Lower plants, like herbs and bushes, also offer potent cures. Yet, it is the trees which produce many of the most powerful natural substances known for reversing disease. Trees are big, so the medicines they produce are correspondingly powerful. In this book the true greatness of medicines from trees will be revealed. Yet, these trees are not from where the average person thinks. They are not from the Amazon or tropics. Instead, they are from the far northern forests of the sub-arctic region. This is where the most potent and versatile tree medicines can be discovered.

The harsh climate of this region challenges the trees to produce profoundly powerful medicines. Furthermore, from a health point of view this region is not nearly as dangerous as the tropics. Nor is the ecosystem as delicate, that is to human intervention. Thus, in these forests the natural cures can be harvested without thoroughly damaging the environment, as usually occurs in the highly sensitive tropical ecosystems.

All trees in the northern forests are medicinal. One tree which is of particular importance is the birch tree, from which a number of cures can be extracted. Both the white and black birch tree are medicinal. So are the mushrooms which grow upon them. In addition, the northern poplar tree produces powerful medicines. The medicines of these trees are largely the subject of this book. In natural medicine the focus has been on the benefits of herbs and other small plants. Again, trees are powerful beings, plus they are enormous. Thus, the medicines they produce are exceptionally powerful. So are the medicines trapped by many of the fungi which grow on these trees. Actually, these medicines are more powerful than those produced by the type of fungi, which grow on soil.

Besides pine and fir trees poplar trees, as well as white birch trees, predominate in North America. It is curious that the white or silvery tree is the source of highly potent medicines. It is as if its whiteness is a sign of purity. Actually, the whiteness is proof of a rich sterol content. This is a kind of dull or pastel white, which is a sign of valuable medicine. A shiny white coating represents the opposite, and in wild plants this may indicate a poison, for instance, the glossy/shiny white berries of the baneberry plant.

In the case of trees a whitish coating is a positive indication. It is the powdery white substance or whitish reflection that is telling. It tells of the existence of potent medicines, which exist in the white layers—the outer bark of birch and poplar trees. These medicines are also found in the buds and leaves. However, the highest concentration is found in the bark. This is because the bark protects the tree from all distress. The key components are in the powdery or dull-white outer bark. Here are found oxygen-rich antioxidants, including sterols, such as betulin and betulinic acid, and flavonoids such as resveratrol and ellagic acid. The latter are more correctly known as ellagotannins. Such flavonoids/ellagotannins also account for the dull whitish glistening seen on wild purple fruit such as wild blackberries, blueberries, black raspberries, and grapes. Even so, the presence of these antioxidants in birch bark largely accounts for its potency. ORAC testing, which is the state-of-the-art system for evaluating antioxidant powers, proves that pulverized wild birch bark is exceedingly powerful. It scores some 1180 per gram, which makes it more powerful as an antioxidant than vitamin E or C and far more powerful than the much touted berries such as blueberries and acai.

People may not realize it, but in the wild it is not only fruit and greens which serve as food for wild creatures, but it is also tree parts. For instance, much of the birch tree is edible. Animals take advantage of this by munching in particular on the buds and early twigs. These keep the animals vital by providing much nourishment plus healing medicines. Now, because of the vast power of the birch tree—as well as its associated fungi—humans are also beginning to gain these benefits.

Even so, for humans this is not a novel finding. Since antiquity the inner bark has been used by the Native Americans as food. Today, research is proving the basis of this. In ancient Siberia the tree was virtually worshiped by the natives. Regardless, the signs are obvious for all to see. There is nothing more beautiful or distinct in nature than a strand of birch trees with their inviting white bark amidst evergreens. Nor is there any sign of greater significance for the human race than the relatively unknown medicines concentrated in this species of tree. This is because within the white substances of this bark are powerful medicines of immense value for humankind. These are medicines which are capable of curing diseases for which, previously, humankind knew none. This is the power of the forest cures mentioned throughout this book.

Let us further investigate birch trees. In that white layer of these trees is a highly medicinal substance known as betulin. It is betulin which has proven to be one of the most powerful anticancer substances known. It is also a potent substance for modulating, that is balancing, the immune system. Additionally, betulin speeds the healing of tissues as well as helps reduce inflammation. Furthermore, it is a natural preservative, as is proven by the fact that birch bark greatly resists decomposition. This is the compound made by the trees for survival. Humans can take advantage of this by consuming it. Moreover, betulin and its associated compounds are exceedingly safe for human intake, that is they can be consumed with impunity. Furthermore, there are no drug interactions with birch bark or its extracts.

However, rather than the bark the most potent cure is a growth on it. This growth concentrates all the bark's medicinal powers. Plus, it essentially pre-digests this bark. This is the chaga mushroom. This mushroom is an exceedingly powerful natural medicine. Chaga has a vast history as a natural medicine and has been used by the primitives for thousands of years. Of note the infamous iceman of the Alps, frozen in a glacier for over 5,000 years, was found in possession of chaga.

What is so unique in this birch tree growth that would elevate it to this status? It was regarded as an invaluable natural drug by the early primitives, that is as early as the Bronze Age. Furthermore, the ancient Chinese and Siberians gave it the highest status of all natural medicines.

What is so potent in its chemistry that would give it this grand status? Foremost of these powers are the plant sterols betulin and betulinic acid. Yet, in the process of feeding on the birch tree it produces its own wild medicines, notably superoxide dismutase (SOD). The latter is one of the most powerful antioxidative enzymes known. SOD is essential for the function of all human cells. In its absence the body degenerates.

Somehow, without any scientific studies this was naturally discovered. In ancient times people in Siberia, China, Korea, and eastern Europe determined that this mushroom is a significant medicine. Even today in Siberia, Russia, Korea, Japan, and eastern Europe, as well as in parts of northern Canada, chaga is used as a therapeutic agent.

Chaga: Supreme of all tree medicines

Chaga is a wild mushroom. Yet, unlike most wild mushrooms instead of growing in the soil or upon decomposing matter it grows on living trees. It has a predilection for birch trees, and it is this birch-growing fungus that is the subject of much of this book. The fungus feeds on and, therefore, concentrates the therapeutic compounds found in birch trees. Thus, it is merely the means to predigest the birch tree nutrients—and medicines—to make them more readily available and to concentrate them in a usable form. In this respect it truly is a divine gift, because it is a vital chemical factory of potent substances, which are of immense value to human health.

The mushroom is kind of an enigma. On the one hand it helps the tree, because, largely, it grows on wounds or weak spots to strengthen it. Yet, ultimately, as it concentrates all the trees' powers it causes them to die. Even so, this is only a part of nature, because chaga only does this to mature trees, which are near death regardless.

Technically, chaga is a polyspore fungus. This means it has a different structure than the typical soil-growing fungi. The latter have gills, while chaga has pores. Another unique feature is that this is a highly dry mushroom, whereas most other mushrooms are soggy or wet. Chaga holds little water in the wild, which is why it is so nutrient dense. Its rich supply of nutrients is largely derived from the birch tree and particularly its bark, which it consumes and concentrates.

No doubt, chaga mushroom is a disease-fighting powerhouse. This mushroom is highly regarded in Russia and eastern Europe as a cancer cure. Here, it has been used for at least 400 years in the reversal of this disease, particularly stomach and lung cancer. The Siberians also hold it as a secret for long life and physical stamina. Too, in northern Canada the Ojibway hold it as a cure for various tumors. For this tribe it is a favored cancer cure. In Europe it has been used to cure inflammatory skin diseases such as eczema and psoriasis. In Korea it is known for its capacity to fight stress and regulate energy. This demonstrates that this natural medicine is highly versatile for the improvement of human health. Moreover, since it is a kind of food—an edible medicinal mushroom—it is entirely safe for human use. It is even safe to consume for those taking numerous medications. Rather, for such individuals it is unsafe not to take it, since chaga mushroom stabilizes the body against the noxious effects of chemical toxins such as those found in pharmaceutical drugs.

Mushrooms have been used as medicine and food from the most ancient times. For countless centuries the Chinese have treasured them as health aids. A number of Chinese herbal potions contain certain mushrooms, which, after drying, are boiled into an infusion. In ancient Egypt the Pharaohs considered mushrooms delicacies, while the Greeks regarded them as strength-foods for their athletes and soldiers. The Romans gave them a divine-like status, serving them in special feasts. Thus, in earlier times many people held mushrooms as having virtual magical properties for the creation of super-human strength. This was because, in fact, certain of these mushrooms, with their nutritional density and their content of potent agents for empowering the immune system, do create a kind of superior health. Plus, many of the mushrooms are rich in molecules, sterols, that are similar to the powerful steroids produced by the human body. With the ingestion of such substances there is a sense of physical strength, which includes an actual increase in muscular power.

In a sense mushrooms are mysterious. They sometimes grow overnight. They are clearly different than any other living entity. Neither plant nor animal they are a category entirely to themselves. Where there is no life, they grow. They thrive on dead and dying matter, mere long ago dead trunks of logs or other decaying matter. Wherever there is rot, mushrooms thrive.

To survive in such an environment mushrooms produce a number of protective substances. These substances include enzymes, antioxidants, and antibiotics. There is also a kind of biological force that allows mushrooms to survive in the most challenging of environments. It is also a force which is needed for the mushroom's main function, which is to seal all damage to aging birch trees. This force is trapped in chaga. Moreover, the nature of the force is unknown, that is it cannot be isolated. However, as is proven by the power it creates when consumed by humans, it is real and absolute. This is the power of existence, the rapid growth capacity, the aggressive ability to produce digestive enzymes, the vast capacity to synthesize antioxidant enzymes, such as SOD, the ability to synthesize large amounts of sterols, and the capacity to make invaluable antibiotics. This is why the health benefits of this tree mushroom are vast. For these reasons chaga is unique among tree mushrooms. Tree mushrooms are particularly desirable, since these are the strongest type. Additionally, there is less sensitivity to this type than the mushrooms which typically grow on the ground.

Perhaps the fact that certain mushrooms are powerful—and effective—is not so mysterious. Who now leads the world in productivity? Is it not the regular mushroom consumers? It is Russia, China, Japan, and Korea which are largely in the forefront. In all such lands the consumption of medicinal mushrooms, including chaga, is virtually routine. In contrast, only a small percentage of people in the Western countries regularly consume medicinal mushrooms. Nor are mushrooms used in modern medicine as standard medical therapy for degenerative diseases, as they are commonly in the Orient. Thus, in Western countries medical doctors have no experience in their use. The consequences of this are dire, since medicinal mushrooms are both safe and effective in the prevention, as well as treatment, of degenerative disease.

Ancient and modern cures

In Chinese medicine among the mass of herbs and potions chaga held an exceptionally high status. As early as 4500 years ago this forest cure was named "A gift from God." It was also called "King of the Herbs." These early Chinese practitioners used chaga for decontamination of the body as well as to support immune function. It was also known by these ancients to contribute to longevity.

In the mountain villages of Siberia even today people rely on chaga. They drink a pulverized form in hot water as a beverage, much like Westerners drink coffee. For respiratory disorders they burned it and inhaled the smoke. For rashes, cuts, and contusions they apply it topically. They also did so for skin rashes. Yet, it was not merely a village medicine. Throughout Tsarist Russia it was the preferred natural medicine of kings and royalty.

This carried through to modern times. Consider a simple fact. As a rule the Russians are a strong, vigorous people. For instance, in many sports they hold the world strength records. Russia is second only to America in global power. Perhaps chaga accounts for the renowned stamina of the Russian people, including their athletes. In the height of their empire Russian wrestlers and weight lifters were virtually impossible to defeat. For instance, in the Olympics of the 1960s through 1980s these athletes were nearly always the most powerful weight lifters and wrestlers. Americans would put their best men against them, and the Russians would still categorically defeat them. Their power was legendary. Chaga was one of the reasons for their stamina, although they largely kept this a secret.

On a daily basis people of the Siberian mountains still consume chaga. They do so to maintain their strength and vitality. As proof of its powers even in the pre-modern era many of these people lived to be in their late 90s and even well over 100. This is a significant achievement, considering the harsh climate in which they live. In contrast, consider the Inuit, who lived to be on average no older than the mid-50s. The main difference between these people is the Siberians' intake of chaga, a food unknown to the Inuit.

The most common use by these villagers is dietary or preventive, that is to maintain a strong immune system and prevent degenerative disease. Yet, still, in Siberia chaga extract is a respected medicine for serious respiratory disorders, such as asthma, bronchitis, and pneumonia, as well as degenerative conditions, particularly gastric/duodenal ulcers, cancer, and tuberculosis. The Russian government supports this. It was the Russian Medical Research Council which has distributed great praise for chaga, deeming it effective in the maintenance of good health as well as in the normalization of immunity and metabolism. This Council has also deemed the mushroom effective in high blood pressure. Few other natural medicines have ever earned such a status.

Even so, it is not as if medicinal mushrooms are available in massive quantities. It would be difficult to serve the whole world with them. This is particularly true of chaga. Yet, through hard work these mushrooms can be found and harvested in nature for the creation of high-grade nutritional supplements. Every dose of such supplements should be treasured as in the wild these mushrooms are rare.

It is important that, in particular, chaga be carefully harvested. Here, there must be no greed, and a certain amount must be left in conservation. The types of products mentioned in this book are picked by people who are educated in conservation and who never over-pick nor destroy nature. This is a requirement for the production of the chaga extracts described here, which are made from the mushroom harvested in the far reaches of the northern wilderness. Regardless, much of it is wasted by clear-cutting and, then, when it is found on mature trees, it must be harvested.

Chaga and similar forest mushrooms are fungi. Thus, rarely, it may not be tolerated. Yet, this is extremely rare if not unknown. For people who are sensitive to mushrooms, perhaps, the chaga may be taken as sublingual drops emulsified in spice oils. In this form it is virtually universally tolerated. The emulsification process not only makes the mushroom components more digestible, but it also neutralizes some of the fungus nature of this mushroom, making it more tolerable, although with chaga there is little if any of this fungal sensitivity. Even so, forest mushrooms are whole foods, which are well tolerated. In fact, of all mushrooms those which grow on trees are the most innocuous of the various edible fungi. Regardless, the vast majority of people find emulsified chaga invaluable for increasing their stamina and physical power, a benefit that all people need.

Tree mushrooms include shiitake, oyster, reishi, maitake, and chaga. Such mushrooms extract the power and strength of the trees, which, after these foods are ingested, is transferred to humans. Trees are among the most powerful of all living entities. It is through the ingestion of the tree mushroom chaga that humans can readily gain the powers of these plants. The birch tree is one of the most long-lived and disease-free of all trees. Chaga concentrates all its greatness.

The trees themselves may be harvested. In the case of birch trees both the inner and outer bark are edible, as are the spring leaves and buds. For poplar the inner bark and spring buds are both food and medicine. Can a mushroom—a fungus—truly be medicinal? The oriental use alone proves this. Regardless, this is obviously the case, since some of the most commonplace medicines today derive from fungi, for instance, penicillin, griseofulvin, erythromycin, and cyclosporine. No wonder T. A. Ajith said in his investigation on medicinal mushrooms, published in the *Journal of Clinical Biochemistry and Nutrition*, that these 'foods' are "unlimited sources of therapeutically useful biological agents." In other words, the mushrooms contain actual substances with potent drug-like actions. Yet, there is a difference between drugs and the mushrooms, since extracts of the latter are free of side effects.

The great threat to human beings from infectious disease and cancer remains preeminent. Rather than vaccines and synthetic drugs only natural medicines, such as chaga, birch bark extract, poplar bud extract, raw honey, and wild oregano oil, offer the hope—and disease-eradicating power—needed by human beings for survival. By taking advantage of these natural medicines the person has not only the opportunity to be protected but also to achieve the cure, which is the eradication of chronic, unrelenting disease as well as protection from sudden life threatening infections.

In this regard medicinal mushrooms have endless potential. Mushrooms contain a wide range of compounds with significant curative properties. Note the authors of the *Pharmacological Potential of Mushrooms* these substances have germ killing properties and are in particular antiviral. They also have significant cancer-killing capacity and clearly help balance, even activate, the immune system. There are compounds in mushrooms which halt and reverse allergy and still others which protect the liver from noxious damage. Other capacities include the ability to reverse pancreatic damage and lower excessively high blood sugar levels. There are also well established pain-relieving and antiinflammatory actions of medicinal mushrooms. Thus, essentially, these mushrooms are cure-alls.

The king of these mushrooms, chaga, is, perhaps, the most rare. It doesn't grow virtually everywhere, like many other forest mushrooms. For the chaga hunter it may take days or even weeks of searching to find one mature growth. So, it must be regarded as a most precious natural medicine to be used conservatively, that is as needed. The best way to use it is in combination with a whole body regeneration plan, including wholesome diet, exercise, and good mental attitude. The intake of birch bark extracts helps conserve it, because to a degree birch bark duplicates it. Do make use of it, but do so with gratitude and care. Also, people should take advantage of wild, raw berries extract, the type made from remote-source Canadian berries (see *The Wild Berry Cure*, Knowledge House Publishers, same author). Chaga and the wild berries make an ideal grouping of natural medicines for prevention of disease and for the maintenance of ideal health.

Chaga and birch bark medicines are most effective in people who don't abuse themselves. There is no use in taking such a powerful natural medicine, while acting destructively. The person should have a positive attitude with the chaga and birch bark, as these are powerful and, therefore, will aid in rebuilding overall health.

Most of the cure is in belief. This is why a positive attitude is so crucial. It makes no sense to take such a precious medicine with a negative attitude. This defeats the purpose. This includes people who repeatedly batter themselves psychologically. In other words, there needs to be a certain degree of peace in a person's heart and soul to most greatly benefit from it. There is another caveat. This is the fact that by taking these natural medicines there is less likelihood to commit self-abuse. When a person feels good—when such a one has his own internal energy—then, this person is less likely to submit to noxious foods and beverages for stimulation and/or energy. By creating internal power the forest medicines will replace this, and, then, when a person returns to the noxious agents, he/she will find that they disrupt the system. As a result, the person will be repelled by such poisonous substances.

This information is life-changing. Now, there can be internal energy like never before experienced. This is the energy needed to rebuild the body and to maintain ideal health. It is also that much desired energy to function ideally on a daily basis. Thus, with chaga-birch bark extracts there is no longer any need for harsh substances, that is foods and beverages that are drug-like. These foods/beverages with noxious and stimulatory effects include coffee, black tea, green tea, cocoa, chocolate, vanilla bean, and cocoa bean. These substances are commonly used by people for an artificial lift. The problem is that people are often addicted to such stimulants. Moreover, they may be allergic to them, which causes inflammation. There are other negative effects such as irritability, spastic colon, sinus inflammation, headaches, heartburn, and excess diuresis. Yet, all these can be replaced with chaga/birch bark. The benefit is the creation of natural physiological energy. This is a kind of power-energy which stimulants are incapable of producing. Thus, through the intake of wild, raw forest medicines, including chaga mushroom extract, birch bark extract, poplar bud extract, wild, raw greens extracts, organic root, and wild, raw berries extracts there is the benefit of the creation of real power, which sustains the individual. In particular is the power of extracts of chaga and birch bark, along with maca. These will replace artificial stimulants and will create such profound powers in the body that were never before experienced. That is the guarantee of the wild forest cures.

Chapter One

Forest Medicines

In North America there is a Shangri La of natural medicine that few people realize. Or, perhaps, it is more correct to deem this a true Fountain of Youth. Now, the potential for prolonged youth is no longer disregarded. This is because it is well established that life expectancy can be positively influenced by the person's habits and nutrition. Regular exercise is surely a key. Yet, so is the intake of healthy food and water. Plus, certain foods or food-like substances are directly related to a long life, in particular, aromatic spices, dark nutritious greens, organic or wild fruit, organic raw milk, naturally occurring antioxidants, wild herbs, and more.

Recently, there has been much discussion of the medicines of nature. There is significant investigation and research, as well as documentaries, regarding the source for such medicines plus their potential for the treatment of disease. Here, usually, to discover the cure the emphasis has been on the most remote, difficult to access parts of the world—and also the most dangerous. Thus, the focus has been on the Amazon and similar tropical regions. While these regions produce spectacular plants and many highly regarded medicines there is an area of equal if not greater importance, which has been neglected. This is the far northern forests of Russia, Europe, and, particularly, North America. In these regions are found among the most potent, reliable medicines of the world. Plus, these regions are easier to access, without as much danger.

So, the northern forest is equally as valuable if not more so as a source of natural medicines as the tropical ones. One reason is the weather. Actually, the harsh climate of the far north creates more powerful medicines than the more mild climate of the deep tropics. There are thousands of northern-source medicines. Here, only a few are described. The northern forest natural medicines described in this book include:

- wild, raw berries and their extracts (kept in a raw state, so the enzymes are intact)
- wild, raw forest greens extracts
- wild chaga mushroom as either an expresso or emulsified raw drops
- wild, raw birch bark concentrate/extract
- wild, raw poplar bark concentrate
- wild, raw poplar bud extract

There is a romance about the northern forest. It is quiet and peaceful. Other than a few relatively timid birds and the occasional hoot of an owl there are no animals screeching. The majority of animals in these forests attempt to escape any human interaction.

It is possible to learn from these animals. This is through observing their eating habits. Animals are instinctive, an attribute which humans sometimes lack. Thus, animals can guide humans regarding what is healthy and what is suspect. They may also guide them regarding what part of a plant is edible and which part is not—or which is inferior. Yet, not everything consumed by animals is fully edible for humans. Even so, by observing them there is much that can be learned about the power of nature.

In wild nature certain animals love tree food. Deer are an obvious example. They thrive by nibbling on new growth of trees, especially the buds and fresh, sprouting growth of twigs. They nip off only the fresh, tender growth. In particular, in the far north they love the buds/tender twigs of pin cherry, saskatoon, and birch trees.

Regarding poplar beaver thrive on this, eating the early twigs and buds but also stripping the bark, particularly from freshly fallen trees.

Poplar is a fast-growing tree. For growth it produces hormone-like substances. These hormone-like substances are concentrated in the tree's inner bark and also buds. This may explain a fact published in a monograph by the U. S. forest service, which is that "Many kinds of animals use (poplar twigs) for food." Specifically, "Moose, elk, and deer" are mentioned as eating poplar stems. The mention of these animals is insightful, since these are powerful creatures. The degree of strength of their muscles is obvious, as is their stamina, as is the beauty of their shape. Thus, humans must take advantage of this knowledge for their own benefit. This is through the consumption of extracts of poplar buds and, perhaps, bark. Regardless, a person must respect the animals for knowing precisely what in the forests are the most powerful medicines for their health, an instinct largely lacking in the human, supposedly the most intelligent being of all.

Chaga: the most powerful of all forest medicines

Throughout history humans have discovered natural medicines, largely through experimentation. This is surely true of chaga mushroom as well as white birch bark. Just when these potent tree medicines were first discovered is unknown. Yet, what is known is that they have been in use as both food and medicine for thousands of years. In particular, Siberian tribes-people realized that chaga mushroom is not only a tasty, soothing beverage but that it also helps maintain good health. Additionally, discovered over the centuries that specific diseases, notably lung conditions, gastrointestinal disorders, infections, skin diseases, and cancer, respond to chaga. Furthermore, they determined, its regular intake had significant preventive effects and was clearly associated with a long and vigorous life.

Yet, how could this mushroom possess such broad-spectrum powers? How could a single living entity, a mere tree mushroom, which grows preferentially on birch trees, have such profound effects, far more than the greatest scientists have achieved? Here is a natural medicine which is more broad in its powers than any pharmaceutical drug— and these actions were known long before the establishment of modern research. Plus, unlike pharmaceutical agents it has no side effects, unless the generation of excellent health is considered such an effect. By mere observation and experience its potency became renowned without massive double-blind studies.

This tremendous power can be understood by reviewing its chemical nature. So, the proof is in the chemistry and nutritional density. Thus, it is no surprise that modern research confirms that the traditional powers of chaga mushroom and its extracts are very real.

Chemistry of chaga and other forest cures

The best way to understand the powers of tree medicines, particularly the chaga mushroom, is to evaluate the chemistry. Chaga is a top source of a wide range of nutrients. Like other fungi it is also rich in enzymes. Yet, it is not the nutrients or the typical digestive enzymes that makes this mushroom unique. Chaga contains massive amounts of the enzyme superoxide dismutase (SOD), which is rarely found in any edible substance. This enzyme acts to absorb noxious free radicals before they can damage the body. Chaga contains 25 to 50 times more SOD than other medicinal mushrooms. This makes it the top source of this enzyme known.

Chaga also contains substances known as sterols in great amounts. These are the plant form of steroids, the latter being made by humans and various animals. So, to reiterate plants synthesize sterols, while humans synthesize steroids. The key sterols in chaga are lanosterol, betulin, lupeol, inotodiol, and betulinic acid. The combination of sterols, particularly those of the betulin family, plus SOD makes chaga unique. It derives the betulin and betulinic acid from the birch bark Plus, apparently, it also synthesizes these. Regarding its rich supplies of SOD, this is produced by the mushroom itself.

For the survival of birch trees, as well as chaga mushroom, in harsh nature both sterols and SOD are required. Yet, too, both are essential for the survival of humans, especially those who are enduring great stress or suffering from chronic disease. Also, extracts of birch bark and. particularly, chaga mushroom are a kind of protective natural medicine for those living in cold climates. After all, the purpose of these natural complexes is to protect the trees upon which they grow. Regardless, sterols, substances similar to the cholesterol in human bodies, and SOD are two of chaga's main constituents. Other major components include saponins, triterpenes (which are also steroid-like), proteins, amino acids, polysaccharides, major minerals, such as calcium and magnesium, and trace minerals.

The production of SOD is a major issue. This is a potent antioxidant system of vast use for the human body. Its ingestion through chaga extracts is essential for the enhancement of human physiology. With age, synthesis declines, as do tissue levels. This may explain the ultimate result of the ingestion of chaga extracts, which is the halting of the aging process. With the regular intake there is a likelihood that lifespan can be extended by as much as 10%, perhaps more. Plus, because of the potent effects of both SOD and sterols there is the benefit of youthfulness. Both these substances block oxidative damage of the tissues. This largely accounts for the significant anti-aging properties of chaga mushroom. White birch bark extract also has this effect, since this is a top source of a wide range of sterols which possess anti-degenerative and antitumor properties.

How crucial is SOD? According to Noguchi and Niki in *Antioxidant Status, Diet, Nutrition, and Health* this enzyme is essential for halting tissue damage. This damage is the result of aberrant forms of oxygen known as reactive oxygen species. This is where SOD is crucial. It is a potent neutralizer of such noxious, destructive oxygen compounds, which result from normal cellular processes as well as inflammation. SOD converts dangerous forms of oxygen, the kind which are so explosive that they can damage and/or destroy cells, to oxygen gas, the type which is breathed. This is why this molecule is essential to life. Moreover, aging is the result of tissue damage, so by blocking this lifespan is extended.

SOD is so essential to this process that it is, clearly, associated with long life. A number of studies have demonstrated the danger of low tissue SOD levels. Such low levels are not only associated with a decline in overall health but are also related to a reduction in lifespan. In contrast, high or normal levels of tissue SOD in the aging body is associated with an increase in lifespan.

Nature tells us this. Chaga is a tree medicine and is the world's top SOD source. Then, what are the longest lived of all organisms? It is the trees, which may live as long as 4,000 years.

In humans hundreds of substances have been evaluated and, then, correlated with longevity. There has as a rule been no universal agreement of the findings, that is with one exception. This is SOD levels. In a key study published in 1984 Richard Cutler of the NIH (National Institutes of Health) made the discovery. He determined that in a variety of animals SOD levels are more greatly correlated with a long and vigorous life than any other factor. Interestingly, humans have the highest levels of this enzyme of any mammals, and they are also the longest lived. Notably, the chimpanzee has about half the human levels of SOD and, correspondingly, about half the lifespan.

Cutler looked at a number of theories of long life and largely disproved them, including the supposition that a cold or slow metabolic rate is a factor. Instead, he proved, the tissue production and levels of antioxidant enzymes are a true factor, the levels of SOD being most well correlated. Notes John Colman in his article "SOD—the Enzyme that Keeps Us Alive in an Oxygen-Rich Atmosphere" the studies proving the definitive role of SOD in anti-aging are "voluminous." This is through the fact that "by-products of oxygen utilization are the main contributors of aging and disease—superoxide radicals, hydrogen peroxide and hydroxyl radicals."

SOD attacks these by-products. It neutralizes such noxious molecules by converting them to mere oxygen and water. Other enzymes which assist the process of neutralizing dangerous free radicals include catalase, peroxidase, and glutathione peroxidase.

These are the essential antioxidant enzymes produced within the body. Notes Colman, "These endogenous (internally produced) enzymes are vastly more potent than dietary antioxidants, such as vitamin C. SOD, for example, is 3,500 times more potent than vitamin C at reducing superoxide radical."

Thus, it is no surprise that when levels of SOD decline, there is a dramatic change in the body. Now, the incidence of degenerative diseases rises dramatically. Without SOD there is no means for the body to neutralize destructive free radicals. Thus, essentially, the body begins to decay; there is no way the organs can fend off the free radicals on their own, that is without sufficient SOD.

Eating increases the production of free radicals, while food restriction and, particularly, fasting stalls this. Yet, most people are not about to cut back on their eating. This is why chaga is an ideal alternative to, for instance, regular fasting, although the use of this mushroom plus such fasting is even more ideal.

Colman also says that, genetically, SOD levels can vary greatly by as much as 50% in humans. This helps explain how "some people are prone to degenerative diseases early in life as opposed to others who lead disease-free lives." Normally, levels of antioxidant enzymes decline with age, while levels of inflammatory gene expression, such as COX-2 and IL6, increase. Colman also notes that there is an exception to this, which is calorie restriction. Experiments in mice, monkeys, and humans have proven that calorie restriction can increase lifespan by as much as 50%. Says Colman, experiments have shown that "animals fed normally one day and deprived of food the next day also lived 50% longer. Human experiments with calorie restriction at 50% daily intake or eating on alternate days also maintained youthful antioxidant enzyme levels and youthful expression of inflammatory genes."

There are two ways to alter SOD levels. One is to take a top natural source such as chaga. Another is to take substances/foods which boost the body's production of this enzyme. Says Colman, "The most promising natural compound has been found in broccoli extracts: D3T (1,2-dithiole, 3-thione). It not only raises SOD and all the other endogenous antioxidants (catalase, glutathione peroxidase and glutathione), it also raises the enzyme glutathione transferase, which neutralizes the toxic metabolites formed by the liver."

The basis for this, notes Colman, is profound: "When this compound is available or found in higher concentrations in broccoli or other natural cruciferous vegetables, it will solve two huge anti-aging problems—the problem of SOD production within the human body and the production of stage II liver enzymes, which will reduce cancers by neutralizing the carcinogens formed during stage I liver detoxification."

With aging it is inevitable that levels of these enzymes decline. Yet, in particular the decline in SOD is devastating. Without it, noxious forms of oxygen run amok. This is critical, because the explosive forms of oxygen readily cause cell damage. This is by causing direct damage to the cell walls, a process known as oxidation. "Lipids are oxidized," note Noguchi and Niki, by reacting with "oxygen molecule(s) quite rapidly to give lipid peroxyl radical." This, they note, causes damage to fats within the cells and in the cell walls, which they call "spoilage," and the damage caused by these rapidly acting free radicals is a proven factor in the cause of degenerative disease of the arterial walls known as atherosclerosis.

The membranes contain cholesterol and phospholipids as key components. These crucial components may be readily damaged through free radical strikes. This causes contortions in the cell membranes. The cells, then, can no longer function. Nor can they defend themselves against attack. As a result, the cells and organs are greatly weakened. Thus, disease readily develops, including heart disease, diabetes, atherosclerosis, arthritis, skin disorders, lupus, and cancer.

SOD halts this toxicity. Yet, here is the danger. The investigators said the poisoning happens suddenly. If there is no or insufficient SOD available, then, the damage proceeds unchecked. Thus, the intake of a daily supplement which provides biologically active SOD is an essential means to prevent or reverse oxygen poisoning in the body. In addition, sterols, as found in the wild chaga, are essential for rebuilding any cell damage, which is caused by oxidative stress. Thus, SOD and the sterols work as a team to both maintain excellent health of the internal organs and also to stall the aging process. This means that SOD- and sterol-rich wild chaga mushroom extracts are ideal for the regeneration of the body and also for the prevention of its degeneration.

SOD: key component

The chemistry of SOD is worthy of a thorough review, because this enzyme alone explains much of chaga's unique properties. Superoxide dismutase is the main enzyme responsible for the destruction of the oxygen free radical, known as superoxide radical, written biochemically as O_2^-. Thus, it protects the cells of the body responsible for metabolizing oxygen from free radical-induced damage. It does so by acting more aggressively and more quickly than the radicals, in other words, it neutralizes them before they can do damage. Thus, SOD is essential to life itself. Without it, it is impossible to have good health. In fact, in its absence the tissues radically degenerate.

SOD was one of the first substances studied by anti-aging pioneer J. McCord, who found that this enzyme protects the tissues from being corrupted by radical oxygen. Unprotected, the violent forms of oxygen cause a phenomenon known as depolymerization, which means, essentially, that the normal structural bonds between human cells are damaged and even destroyed.

This enzyme is found in all human, as well as animal, tissues. The best dietary sources include chaga mushroom, other medicinal mushrooms, green peas, cabbage, dark green leafy greens, nutritional yeast, wheat grass, wheat germ, beef heart, and raw liver. Of note, nearly all medicinal mushrooms are rich in this enzyme but chaga is by far the highest. SOD's role in preserving the health of the body is vast. This again relates to the O_2- ion, which according to an article by Worthington Biochemical is "important in aging, lipid peroxidation, and the peroxidative hemolysis of red blood cells...". In other words, this form of oxygen causes destruction of tissue, including the systematic destruction of red blood cells. Noxious oxygen is produced in part by the natural metabolic processes. Oxygen is used to burn fuel, the latter being derived from food. It is also produced as a result of exposure to radiation, either from X-rays, CT-scans, or excessive exposure to sunlight. Regardless, destruction of tissue is synonymous with aging, whereas the blockage of this process is equivalent to youthfulness.

The enzyme itself is a great blessing for human beings. It is the blessed creator who made this special complex for protecting the human body from disease and, particularly, excessive aging. There is a critical point, however, where levels decline naturally with age, resulting in a corresponding increase in the aging process. People should take advantage of this and increase the consumption of SOD-rich foods, especially after 50. Chaga mushroom extract is the top source of naturally occurring SOD known. Again, if the enzyme is in complete decline, aging proceeds rapidly. In fact, in genetically-induced aging syndromes, where people age at a highly accelerated rate, the levels of this enzyme are nil. Thus, this is the most crucial complex for the prevention of aging of the body. The point is the production of toxic forms of oxygen is unavoidable. Without SOD the human body would be decimated within a few short years.

SOD has the specific role of dealing with superoxide radical and is highly capable of doing so. No other component of the human body can achieve this. SOD miraculously attracts this noxious molecule by acting as a kind of platform for its absorption, so it can be rendered into relatively harmless oxygen (regular O_2) and hydrogen peroxide. This is known as the "collision" of superoxide radical with SOD. In a most magnificent mechanism SOD relentlessly seeks out toxic forms of oxygen. It hunts this oxygen, incredibly, just as it form so it can attack and neutralize it. The fact is it is genetically designed to do so.

Regarding its biological effects SOD, either ingested or used topically, blocks certain elements of aging. One of these elements is known as fibrosis, which is a kind of degeneration of connective tissues. The best way to gain these effects is through the use of food sources of this enzyme, since dietary supplements containing SOD are largely ineffective. This may explain the well established anti-aging effects of many of the aforementioned foods such as raw liver, beef heart, medicinal mushrooms, wheat grass, cabbage/sauerkraut, and dark leafy greens. This is why chaga mushroom is so invaluable, because not only is it an exceedingly rich source of this enzyme, but it also offers it in a form that can be utilized. This is true whether taken topically or internally. To gain the power of natural SOD humans should consume chaga as an emulsion. Here, it should be taken as sublingual drops, which further bolsters absorption. Also, it may be consumed as a kind of expresso, or hot tea combined with wild white birch bark.

To further enhance SOD levels beef or bison hearts can be consumed, along with dark leafy greens, fresh organic peas, raw cabbage, medicinal mushrooms, and nutritional yeast. Some people prefer wheat grass as a source of the enzyme, and its rich content of SOD may explain the profound effects on the body by its regular consumption. For those who are sensitive to wheat the aforementioned vegetables and, particularly, the chaga are ideal alternatives.

Oxygen: essential nutrient or poison?

Everyone knows that oxygen is potent. It is the most reactive—the most flammable—of all gases. In the body this toxicity doesn't come from gaseous oxygen but, rather, from one of its molecular by-products known as superoxide. This is why the body makes billions of molecules daily of an enzyme to destroy this—superoxide dismutase—which catalyzes the destruction of the superoxide free radical.

This free radical, if left unopposed, attacks healthy tissue. Here, the tissue is distorted and even split apart. At a minimum the free radicals cause inflammation. The maximum damage is represented as the onset of disease, as well as rapid aging, including age-related damage to the skin.

Medicinal mushrooms are the top known sources of this substance. A chart of the SOD content of such mushrooms was published by Japan's Tokyo-based Research Department of Health and Food Products. Here, the real truth regarding chaga is revealed. SOD content of six mushrooms was evaluated with the most incredible results conceivable. While well known mushrooms, such as maitake and reishi, are high in this potent enzyme, chaga is massively higher. Here are the numbers: reishi and maitake each score 4200 enzyme units per three grams (a typical serving), while chaga scores 105,000. Thus, this mushroom is some 24-fold higher than any other. This means that from a nutritional and biological point of view this tree mushroom truly is the king of all fungi.

Unlike the majority of medicinal fungi a person doesn't eat this mushroom. Rather, it is taken as a medicine. It can also be used as a food additive for the purpose of a nutritional boost for soup, drinks, or smoothies.

Supplements of SOD are essentially worthless. This is demonstrated by a variety of studies, where SOD was given orally. In all such studies the oral intake of SOD in a supplemental and/or chemical form did not influence tissue levels. Regardless, this is a live, electrically charged substance. Thus, the natural form cannot be duplicated synthetically.

The effective way to consume superoxide dismutase is through whole foods and their extracts. This is largely because of the nature of this molecule. This relates to its electrical charge, which cannot be duplicated artificially. In the raw state such whole foods and/or whole food extracts retain their biological charge. This demonstrates the value of the emulsified whole food chaga extract, which is a raw emulsion in extra virgin olive oil, as well as the hot water infusion or chaga expresso. Additionally, wild, raw forest greens, as drops under the tongue, provide other oxygenating factors such as the oxygen-metabolizing vitamin riboflavin.

To protect the body from aging, as well as the onset of disease, the intake of whole food concentrates rich in SOD is essential. The only reliable source of highly absorbable SOD is natural concentrates, for instance, the hot water infusion of wild chaga mushroom and/or the emulsified wild chaga drops. Regarding the drops to assist absorption sublingual administration is ideal. Other SOD concentrates include wheat grass juice, raw sauerkraut, broccoli sprouts, and raw or lightly cooked liver.

The function of this enzyme is impressive. It is strictly designed to halt the toxicity of destructive forms of oxygen, particularly the superoxide radical. It bears repeating. In a mechanism that defies human intelligence as quick as these oxygen radicals react SOD reacts even quicker to serve its role of protecting human tissue. If there is plenty of this molecule in human tissues, aging due to oxygen reactions is essentially stalled. This is because if free radicals are being produced and sufficient SOD is available, these aging factors will be neutralized.

The proof of its role in greatly protecting the body is significant. Mice which lack SOD or associated enzymes develop a wide range of diseases, including the relatively rare liver cancer as well as cataracts. Such mice also develop muscle loss at an earlier age than normal and are more sensitive to toxic chemicals than those with a definite SOD status. They also die younger than mice with normal levels. Also, failure to produce sufficient quantities of the enzyme in human brains is associated with increased risk for Lou Gehrig's Syndrome (ALS) as well as Alzheimer's disease. A lack of SOD in the brain, due to mutation, may, in fact, cause this disease. The joints, too, degenerate in the event of the deficiency. As noted by Germano and Cabot in *Nature's Pain Killers* levels of SOD are low in people with arthritis. They are also low in those suffering from inflammatory disorders such as fibromyalgia and polymyositis as well as the highly deforming rheumatoid arthritis. This is further proof that in the event of the deficiency tissue destruction is inevitable.

The triterpenes: building blocks for powerful health

The triterpenes are another critical group of chaga/birch bark active ingredients. These triterpenes are sterols, in other words, they are lipids. The lipids are a kind of wax. Think of them as substances which increase the resistance, that is the strength, of cell membranes, like the waxes, which give strength to the outer peels of apples and berries or the outer layer (bark) of trees. For instance, it is well known that waxes applied to the outside of fruit and vegetables extends their shelf-life. Biological waxes, such as those found in chaga and birch bark, have a similar effect on human cells. These waxes/triterpenes include betulin, betulinic acid, lanosterol, inotodiol, and lupeol. It is these substances which are largely responsible for the cancer killing effects of both birch bark and chaga. Part of this is, again, related to their effects on the cell walls, both of healthy cells and cancerous ones. These are steroid-like molecules made of carbon with a considerable amount of oxygen. They are among the largest and most complex biological molecules known.

Being large molecules, they may be somewhat difficult to absorb, but in a mycelized or emulsified form they are readily absorbed. Once absorbed, these cholesterol-like compounds are extensively utilized by the cells. The triterpenes enter the walls of human cells. The cells then use these steroid-like substances for a wide range of functions, including the maintenance of the health of the cell walls themselves. Healthy cell walls are the greatest immunization against cancer. Here, a healthy cell wall is flexible, while a diseased one is stiff. The flexibility of cell walls is directly related to the sterol (or steroid) content.

Triterpenes also serve as raw materials for synthetic processes. In the adrenal glands, testes, and ovaries these triterpenes are mobilized for the synthesis of key hormones, including adrenal steroids, testosterone, DHEA, estrogenic compounds, and progesterone. The brain absorbs them for use in the regeneration of the nerve cell coating, the latter being known as the myelin sheath. Koyoma notes that these substances have an impact on the fluidity and, therefore, flexibility of human cell membranes, influencing the transmission of signals. Moreover, this is true of all cell membranes in the body. That is why the effects of the ingestion of wild, raw chaga drops is so dramatic as well as diverse.

Some triterpenes are also known as saponins or saponin glycosides, the latter standing for complex molecules made of glucose. Again, these are steroidal, that is cholesterol-like. Like the sterols/triterpenes cholesterol is a wax and is needed for membrane health by all cells in the body. While this molecule is deemed dangerous by the medical profession this is baseless, as it is a natural and essential component of human nutrition. In fact, the fear mongering regarding cholesterol is largely orchestrated by the pharmaceutical cartel in order to sell cholesterol-lowering drugs. It is also to promote the continuous use of tests for cholesterol levels. The latter is proven by the fact that medical companies make untold billions of dollars every year from such relatively useless testing. Then, the tests promote drug therapy, which forcibly lowers cholesterol to dangerously low levels. Yet, routinely, cholesterol levels can be normalized with diet alone, although certain nutritional supplements may also prove productive. One of the most effective of such supplements is a combination of cumin, red sour grape, northern Pacific kelp, and garlic. Search for this at superior health food stores.

As proof against this medical fraud the body makes billions of molecules of cholesterol daily. Thus, forcibly removing it does result in damage. Incredibly, drugs are given to do this, and cholesterol is restricted from the diet, all to the body's detriment. Everyday the human body makes the equivalent of the cholesterol found in two dozen eggs. Here, it is used for a wide range of functions, including the production of vitamin D, the repair of damage to arterial walls, because of its wax-like and sealant properties, the regeneration of cell walls, the re-building of the coatings of nerves, that is the myelin sheath, the building and strengthening of muscle tissue, the production of adrenal hormones, the production of ovarian and testicular hormones, and the synthesis of bile. This is why any drug which vigorously destroys cholesterol will cause damage to the human body. In this regard the cholesterol lowering drugs actually increase the potential not only for by-pass surgery but also for potentially fatal heart disease. The depletion of cholesterol from the body causes hormonal chaos. This can only lead to devastation.

The saponin glycosides, which are found in rich amounts in chaga and other tree mushrooms, have the power known as emulsification. This means that these substances can dissolve certain kinds of fat. In healthy cells they merely make the membranes more fluid, which is of vast benefit to human health. However, in diseased cells, notably the cells of cancerous tumors, this emulsification action serves a different function. This is because, here, these molecules cause the cancer cell membranes to break down or dissolve, somewhat similar to how soap removes grime. Thus, in particular an emulsified form of chaga mushroom extract, available as sublingual drops, is ideal for natural anticancer treatment. Also, a hot water infusion is effective, since this method, too, is a means to emulsify the sterols. The saponin glycosides lend themselves well to this emulsification. Everyone knows that commercial wax readily dissolves in hot water, and the same is true of the natural waxes, that is sterols, as found in the cell systems of chaga mushroom. So, again, both the sublingual drops and the hot water extraction are acceptable forms of this natural medicine.

Such extracts, by directly affecting the cell walls of cancer cells, have a highly positive action. This is through the transmission of electrical impulses in these cells. Compared to healthy cells cancer cells are notoriously weak. Without their ability to communicate they die. Thus, by reducing the capacity of these cells to communicate chaga mushroom extract causes the cells to self-destruct, that process known as apoptosis.

Inotodiol is one of the most abundant triterpenes, that is sterols, in chaga. Some investigators regard it as the most potent one. This substance is a powerful antitumor agent, which has been shown to rapidly cause the death of cancer cells. This is due in part to the capacity of the molecule to dissolve cell membranes. It is also the result of the fact that inotodiol is a powerful source of molecular oxygen, the latter being poisonous to tumor cells.

It is well established that chaga mushroom extracts activate the immune system. This is true of both healthy people and those with chronic disease. In all cases the activation, perhaps more correctly described as "normalization," of the immune system is positive. This is because in this modern, highly polluted and stressful world peoples' immune systems are greatly impaired. This activation is largely due to the sterols. Even so, another highly powerful component is the polysaccharides. These substances, found in chaga in rich amounts, greatly empower the immune system. The mushroom contains high levels of one of the most potent polysaccharides known, which is beta glucan. This substance is a powerful anticancer agent. There are a number of clinical studies which demonstrate beta glucan's vigorous actions against cancer. Its cancer fighting effects derive from the fact that it greatly activates the immune system. Beta glucan also causes a significant reduction in blood sugar in those who suffer abnormal blood sugar peaks.

The substance lanosterol is found in rich quantities in tree mushrooms. The name reveals its structure, *lano-sterol*. Thus, it is a cholesterol-like molecule. Studies show that this substance is anti-viral. Only the wild type of tree mushrooms contain this in rich amounts. Curiously, as reported by Koyoma when this mushroom is grown in vats, the lanosterol content drops 11-fold. Thus, there is no way to make these mushrooms artificially, that is while simultaneously retaining their medicinal properties. It is the mushroom in a whole food form—the wild remote-source mushroom—which is medicinally active. Here, as proven by the attempts to synthesize the natural chemistry chaga is obviously unique, being synthesized by the almighty creator in a manner impossible to duplicate. Thus, chaga is made by the One who knows what is of benefit to the human being. This is obvious by its ingestion, because the benefits are vast. Just like it strengthens the trees it also empowers the human body. The point is rather than the laboratory or man-made version the real power is in the natural, wild source, which grows in the forest on birch trees. This is the only chaga which is suitable for human use.

When thinking of the chemistry of chaga, there should be only one consideration, which it is that natural complex which creates a strong, vital body. This is by the enhancement of the immune system. Moreover, the immune system deals with allergy, inflammation, circulation, infection, and detoxification as well as the prevention of cancer. Thus, all humans would benefit from a more active—or more natural—immune response. Chaga mushroom and to a degree white birch bark provide all the chemicals needed to create such an active immunity, as demonstrated by the powers of the polysaccharides, which are now described in greater detail, as follows:

Beta glucan: potent mushroom polysaccharide

This is perhaps the most potent immune potentiator from mushrooms. It is found in chaga mushroom in dense amounts. The type of this molecule found in chaga is primarily 1, 3 beta glucan (named henceforth for simplicity beta glucan). This substance is renowned for its role in activating the immune system. It may be regarded as a secret weapon for preparing the immune system against any external—and internal—threat. According to Russian investigators beta glucan is such a powerful activator that it essentially prepares the entire immune system—in other words, it readies it—to destroy cancer cells, and also any other aberrant cells, including the cells of skin disorders.

Human research demonstrates the immense power of this substance. In one study people who underwent surgery were treated with beta glucan. This was in the attempt to reduce the incidence of post-surgical infection as well as septic death. The result of the trial was highly significant, in fact, incredibly, this therapy reduced post-operative infections by some 40%. This means that beta glucan-rich substances, notably chaga mushroom, save lives. Again, in humans an experiment was done on trauma patients, who are always at risk for complications and even death. In this study, where beta glucan was administered versus placebo, the results were profound. There were no deaths in the glucan-treated group, while some 30% of the untreated group died. Regarding the development of sepsis, that is blood poisoning, only about 10% of the beta glucan treated patients were stricken, while some 50% of the untreated group succumbed. These are highly impressive results, which prove that this mushroom/yeast extract is truly lifesaving. The beta glucan achieved this by causing the immune system to function at the optimal level. The results also mean that the routine use of beta glucan-rich chaga extracts will extend lifespan significantly, largely by reducing the risks for life-threatening infections as well as by preventing infections in general.

In another study white blood cell powers were evaluated, specifically their ability to attack and consume bacteria was scrutinized. The administration of crude glucan particles by mouth resulted in a significant increase in the ability of white blood cells to consume bacteria. The conclusion was that the consumption of glucan in a whole food state is a good means to strengthen the immune system. This is because the consumption of beta glucan protects the immune system from being overwhelmed by bacteria through causing it to more efficiently destroy them.

In a most incredible finding beta glucan was tested against anthrax. Here, in a study conducted by the Canadian

Department of Defense mice were treated with this substance, with and without antibiotics, for one week. Then, they were infected with anthrax. The mice treated with the beta glucan survived, while those treated with antibiotics alone all died. This intrigued the researchers, so they conducted an additional test, this time giving the beta glucan after infecting the mice. Still, there was great immune power, with some 85% survival in the treated group, while the survival in the control group dropped and was a mere 30%. This is a significant, powerful result, far more so than any drug. Also, an investigation on artificially infected mice, who were contaminated with *Candida albicans*, proved that this substance is anti-yeast. It was discovered that the administration of this compound helped the animals' immune systems clear the yeasts from their bodies, largely by activating the capacity of white blood cells to seek out and destroy these germs.

Even if there is immunosuppression, even if function is compromised by surgical invasion, such as splenectomy, mushroom extracts with beta glucan are effective. Beta glucan simply boosts immunity regardless of the status or circumstance. In mice a study was done to evaluate the protective powers of this substance after splenectomy, since this procedure greatly compromising immunity. Beta glucan "increased survival vs. controls…75% as opposed to 27%." That is virtually a three-fold increase in survival. No drug can achieve this.

If forest cures, rich in beta glucan and other glyconutrients, such as chaga mushroom emulsion, were made available in hospitals in surgical wards, the death rate from secondary infection would plummet. Countless lives would be saved. Dire medical catastrophes would be minimized, perhaps avoided. In other words, premature death would be halted. Furthermore, people undergoing surgery would largely be safe-guarded from dangerous post-surgical infections. The surgical patient would be stronger and would therefore recover quicker. Surgery could be achieved without such a vast degree of catastrophes.

The implications are obvious. Beta glucans improve the body's ability to ward off infection by strengthening the germ-killing capacity of the various immune surveillance cells, including macrophages, Kuppfer cells (in the liver), neutrophils, and natural killer cells. This improved action is against any germ, including bacteria, viruses, fungi, and parasites.

The mechanism of action is quite astounding. Beta glucans are absorbed by the cells which line the gut wall and are, then, transported into the lymph. Here, they interact with macrophages to activate immune function.

This potent effect on blood cells was demonstrated regarding radiation. Mice were administered beta glucan IV and then irradiated. The irradiated mice with beta glucan exhibited a significantly enhanced recovery of radiation-damaged red and white blood cell counts, as well as platelet counts, compared to controls. This proves that beta glucan aided in the regeneration of bone marrow cells, known as megakaryocytes. These cells are needed for the production of new blood cells. There is another benefit to the bone marrow from this substance. This relates to chemotherapy-induced bone marrow suppression or failure. This is where the regenerative cells are virtually exterminated. In one study much of this pathology was reversed, in other words, after administration of the mushroom derivative the bone marrow and blood counts largely returned to normal.

Thus, it becomes obvious that beta glucans have a direct power over the bone marrow. There are few if any other substances which have such a profound action. Allendorf and his group demonstrated that beta glucan as whole molecules, the type found in chaga mushroom, acts to *regenerate the bone marrow* following radiation therapy.

This crude glucan actually accelerates red cell production, known medically as hematopoiesis. Other research has shown that beta glucan stimulates the synthesis of red blood cells in the bone marrow, as well as spleen, in radiation-damaged mice. No other substance known has such profound effects. Moreover, chaga is rich in beta glucan, so it is a must-take substance for anyone exposed to high doses of radiation such as that occurring from CAT scans, radiation therapy, frequent flying, mammography, nuclear power plants, and X-rays.

The glucans are readily desired by the body, so they are actively absorbed. Studies using radioactively-labeled glucan found that after ingestion these particles exist in the bloodstream, meaning they are fully absorbed. There is a massive lymph tissue in the gut, known as the Peyer's patches. It is from here that the glucan molecules are absorbed. Here, they form key functions involved in the systematic regulation of the immune system. Thus, all people living in the modern high-stress world, who are exposed to its many immune system-damaging hazards, should be consuming rich sources of beta glucan such as chaga mushroom.

Fat is needed for this absorption. While the beta glucan can be taken on an empty stomach with much success a bit of animal fat or heavy vegetable fat would assist absorption such as the fat of organic beef, organic butter/cheese, extra virgin olive oil, nuts, nut butter, and/or organic whole milk and whole milk yogurt.

Crude tree mushroom extracts are the preferred source of this substance. There are a number of other beta glucan supplements available, but these are derived through a high degree of processing. The emulsified chaga extract is the whole food approach. In contrast, with the processed types various chemicals are used in their development. Plus, some of the commercial beta glucan supplements are derived from yeast—and certain of these organisms are genetically engineered. This means that commercial beta glucan supplements may contain toxins derived from the genetic engineering process. Thus, while there may be benefits there may also be a degree of toxicity. Truly natural beta glucan, as found in whole mushroom concentrates, is non-toxic. It is also more powerful than the purified form, since there is a synergistic action of the various beta glucan molecules, which is lost with mere isolation of the single molecule. Regardless, be sure any beta glucan supplement is free of genetically engineered components. With chaga this is no issue, since the beta glucan occurring in chaga extracts is naturally occurring.

Humans have only limited knowledge. Natural medicines, such as chaga and other whole food mushrooms, consist of hundreds and in some cases thousands of substances. Moreover, there is no way that a single component or a synthetic one is the same as the whole. No one can understand the interactions, that is the synergy of the group. Single components are isolated and synthesized merely to achieve a patent. In this way the maker has a monopoly. It is never done for health benefits, that is to create a superior—and safer—medicine. To achieve the maximum effect of polysaccharides as medicines the whole crude mushroom extract/concentrate, such as whole emulsified chaga, whole oyster mushroom, whole reishi, and whole maitake, should be consumed. Regarding chaga whole food sources include emulsified chaga drops in a spice oil base and the chaga tea/coffee with wild birch bark and organic black/purple maca.

Nutritional density

Without doubt, forest mushrooms are among the most nutritionally dense of all food sources. In particular, chaga contains a vast array of substances, which are of great value for human nutrition. Some 215 nutrients and/or phytochemicals have been identified in this mushroom. Chaga is so rich in nutrients that it may be regarded as one of the world's top sources of minerals and vitamins. The density of nutrients is critical, particularly for stimulating the healing process. As well, in the treatment of disease a high density of nutrients is essential. Foods, like chaga, which are low in calories but high in nutrients, are clearly associated with an increase in longevity. This nutritional power is so considerable that Xiu-hong Zhong of China's Medical College of Yanbian University simply said that chaga mushroom has a "high nutritional...value" in the treatment of degenerative disease. In particular, he made clear, this nutritional power proves invaluable for the reversal of cancer, heart disease, diabetes, and even AIDS.

The nutrient density of this mushroom is related to its age and also climate. The age allows it to create a vast amount of nutrients through synthesis. The climate places such great stress on it that it produces nutrients for self-protection. Chaga contains virtually every known nutrient. The only primary ones which are missing are vitamin A and vitamin K. There are considerable amounts of B vitamins, particularly pantothenic acid, riboflavin, and biotin. There is B_{12} and the highly rare vitamin D. It contains also a wide range of minerals, including calcium, magnesium, phosphorus, copper, iron, manganese, potassium, and zinc. Additionally, it is a top source of antioxidant enzymes as well as digestive enzymes. Chaga is essentially all nutrients, that is there is no waste. Few foods can match its nutritional powers.

As a rule mushrooms are more nutritionally dense than, for instance, fruit and vegetables. They contain a higher density of amino acids than either vegetables or grains, plus they contain a number of amino acids that are only rarely found in plant matter.

Regarding the exact vitamin and mineral content an analysis was done on wild North American chaga (test done by North American Herb & Spice). This analysis proved that this mushroom is an excellent source of B vitamins and is particularly rich in pantothenic acid, containing nearly a gram per 100 grams. It contains virtually all major and trace minerals and is a particularly good source of potassium, calcium, and magnesium. It even contains B_{12} in trace amounts, which is exceedingly rare for a plant-like growth. Yet, chaga's greatest nutritional density is its content of SOD, which it contains in massive amounts, far greater than any other known food.

There are also novel nutrients in chaga rarely found in any other food. One of these rare nutrients is germanium, which is only found in highly oxygenated foods. Germanium is heavily researched for its ability to improve blood chemistry and boost overall immunity.

Antioxidant powers

Tree medicines are among the most powerful antioxidants known. Trees are big creatures, and so they have more unique means for protection than smaller plants. Birch bark, poplar buds, poplar bark, and chaga mushroom are all powerful antioxidants. Regarding chaga a study was done to evaluate the antioxidant effects. Here, as published in the *Journal of Ethnopharmacology*, January 2005, it was found that chaga has "strong antioxidant activity," this being particularly true of two key components, which are the polyphenols and the steroids (that is sterols). However, there is a caveat: both these substances are relatively difficult to absorb. Rendering them fat soluble assists this process. This has been achieved by one company through a specialized emulsification process, turning the chaga sterols into a well-absorbed cream-like liquid. This illustrates the benefit of taking an extract, as drops under the tongue, which is emulsified with natural emulsifying agents. This process assists the digestion and absorption of the rather difficult-to-absorb cholesterol-like sterols and polyphenol molecules. Through emulsification these molecules are readily transported into the blood through the lymph. Such an extract, concluded the investigators, would be invaluable in human health by acting to "protect cells against oxidative stress."

Free radicals are well established as a cause of disease. Blocking the excessive production of these molecules helps preserve health. It is also a means for the treatment of certain diseases, including heart disease, diabetes, high blood pressure, psoriasis, eczema, lupus, arthritis, hardening of the arteries, heart disease, cancer, and neurological disorders.

While chaga is high in antioxidants the bark and buds of trees are even higher. Consider poplar bud or, rather, its extract. This extract, made exclusively with spice oils, raw vinegar, and extra virgin olive oil, is a powerful agent for fighting pain and inflammation. This is particularly true of the inflammation/pain associated with disorders of the bones, muscles, and joints. This may be due to the fact that extract of poplar bud is a top source of natural antioxidants, which block the inflammatory process. It is also rich in aspirin-like molecules, which directly reverse pain.

The color of chaga, which varies in its layers from rich black to chocolate-colored and, ultimately, yellowish-brown, is telling. Like actual chocolate and carob this is a sign of antioxidant power. In particular, chaga is rich in a complex of antioxidants known as chromogenic complex. While other medicinal mushrooms contain this complex, usually in a minor percentage such as one or two percent, chaga contains this at the incredible level of some 25% of dry weight. These are essentially the pigments, which are highly medicinal. The pigments are phenolic compounds and contain such well established, potent antioxidants as syringic acid, vanillic acid, pyrogallic acid, pyrocatechuic acid, and derivatives of benzoic acid.

The pigments are made by the mushroom to protect it, notably against sunlight as well as the noxious actions of toxic forms of oxygen. When ingested by humans, these pigments have the same action for human cells. Essentially, the aforementioned pigments are types of naturally occurring melanin, the same substance which colors human skin and which, therefore, protects it against sunlight. As a side benefit melanin helps keep the exterior of the body youthful, that is it protects the skin and hair from excessive aging. It even protects the hair from premature graying.

The melanins are highly potent. Chinese investigators at Nanchang University determined that these compounds have "strong antioxidant activity." Specifically evaluating the dark melanin pigments of medicinal fungi Russian investigators publishing in *Applied Biochemistry and Microbiology* deemed them as having "high antioxidant activity," with particular powers in protecting the genes form oxidative damage.

Crude wild birch bark is also high in antioxidant powers. Measurements of wild Canadian-source birch bark show an ORAC level of some 2200 to 2400 per gram. Thus, extracts of wild northern forest trees are the most potent antioxidant supplements known.

Chemistry of birch bark

While chaga mushroom has been the subject of much study due to its anticancer properties the raw material from which it is derived, birch bark, is also highly antitumor. There are two main substances in this bark that have been the subject of study, which are betulin and betulinic acid.

Pharmaceutical companies have concentrated on betulinic acid. They have found a way to extract and concentrate this from the bark. They also semi-synthesize it. In order to concentrate it they use harsh solvents such as methanol. Betulinic acid is a cholesterol-like molecule known as a pentacyclic triterpene. Penta means five, and this refers to the five ring complexes in the molecule. Again, the substance is highly similar to the natural steroids made in the human body. Yet, it is not merely this compound which accounts for the bark's powers. All birch components, those found in the bark and also those concentrated in chaga, are electrically charged. Much of these charged compounds are lipids of the cholesterol family. This makes sense, since steroids and sterols act as conductors of electricity. In the human body, as well as in plants, these molecules act as electron sinks. The electrons create internal energy, which gives the organs the strength to combat disease. This is why plants rich in sterols are usually also highly antitumor. Another reason for the antitumor effect is the wax-like properties of the sterols. Biological waxes stabilize cell membranes, which block tumor invasion.

The coating of the nerves in the brain is made from cholesterol molecules. According to the National Cancer Institute (NCI) the active components of birch bark possess "antiinflammatory, anti-HIV, and antineoplastic activities." Specifically, says the NCI, betulinic acid "induces apoptosis through induction of changes in mitochondrial membrane potential..." This, the organization notes, leads to the production of potent forms of oxygen radicals, and it is these radicals which destroy the cancer cells. These birch bark-induced radicals cause the destruction in part by breaking apart the cancer cells' DNA. There could be no more significant mechanism than this. In fact, it would appear that the whole purpose of white birch, black birch, and chaga mushroom is the programmed destruction of tumor cells.

The emphasis by the NCI and others on betulinic acid is confusing. The reason is that people are led to believe that this is the key curative substance. This is not the case. It is the whole food complex, both of chaga mushroom and whole birch bark, which is truly curative. Historically, these are precisely the forms which have been used and which account for countless cures. Because of the research, including work on patents, people are led to believe that only this single birch bark compound is effective, even though it is heavily refined. This is not the case. In fact, according to investigators in Amsterdam, the Netherlands, the unaltered type, betulin, is capable of killing cancer cells "more rapidly" than the semi-synthetic type. Thus, the crude whole food extract is always preferable to the artificial type. Moreover, the crude or whole food type has the entire complexity of natural substances, which offer synergistic actions, versus the pharmaceutical product, which is simply one synthesized or extracted chemical.

There was an interesting culmination to this study. This is the fact that the birch bark components, notably betulin and betulinic acid, are more active when combined with cholesterol. Thus, an ideal way to consume both the wild-based betulin drops and the chaga expresso are with organic whole milk, cheese, or organic egg yolks, and even natural meats. The Netherlands researchers discovered that cholesterol "sensitized" cells to betulin-induced programmed destruction. Of course, this destruction is only true against diseased cells. Another option is to consume these forest medicines simultaneously with royal jelly. Regardless, the researchers concluded that betulin, the most active ingredient of the whole crude bark, as well as whole chaga mushroom, "has potent anti-tumor activity, especially in combination with cholesterol." This compound is also found in birch bark emulsion, which is taken as drops under the tongue.

Chaga: methods of extraction

Researchers have investigated plants bearing antioxidants such as chaga and tree bark. In these investigations they have found that in order to extract the antioxidants and make them absorbable they must use solvents. The solvents cause the extraction of various lipids, that is sterols and also dissolve the polyphenols, which are among the most powerful antioxidants and antiinflammatory agents known. These substances are somewhat difficult to absorb. The solvent extract particularly of chaga mushroom, they report, has been proven to exhibit "potent antioxidant activity."

Thus, to maximize the power of tree medicines solvents would appear necessary. However, there is toxicity with synthetic chemicals which are used in this regard such as methanol, alcohol, and hexane, the latter being essentially a type of gasoline. All such solvents are highly poisonous to human cells. Surely, they should never be used in the making of natural products. Furthermore, contrary to industry claims their residues can never be completely removed from the final product. Plus, these solvents disrupt the chemistry of natural substances, such as the molecules found in birch bark and chaga, reducing their powers. This demonstrates the need for solvents which are natural and which do not damage the molecules nor the human body. This is why this book promotes the use of tree medicines made through the use of natural extracting substances such as hot water, raw vinegar, extra virgin olive oil, and wild (emulsified) spice oils. The chaga and birch bark emulsions, for instance, are made through the use of such natural substances and are never extracted using toxic chemicals.

Yet, again, the role of solvents is crucial. The term itself means "to dissolve." The reason this is crucial is that the essential medicines of chaga and birch bark, the sterols, are difficult to absorb. Consider the investigations of Korean scientists, who through the use of various solvents extracted five yellow-appearing chaga waxes, which are the sterols (egg yolk is yellow because of animal steroids). These compounds have a ringed structure and consist of carbon and hydrogen, along with much oxygen. Their structure proves that they are vigorous antioxidants of immense value to human cells. Plus, since they are steroid-like waxes, that is lipids, they are directly used within the cells to improve the health of the cell membranes. Any substance with such properties is of value for the reversal of human disease. This is particularly true of disease caused by inflammation and/or degeneration. This is because these waxes are essential for the rebuilding of cell components. They are the primary substances used by the cell membranes. This means both sterols and steroids are essential to all life processes. All organs require them in significant amounts. Even so, unless these waxes can be dissolved much of their powers will be lost.

Again, the sterols of chaga are used by the body as essential cellular components, which demonstrates the massive role of this mushroom in human health. These sterols are both antiinflammatory and antioxidative. There could be no more powerful group of compounds to incorporate into human cells than the tree mushroom sterols. Upon incorporation into the cells these oxygen-rich waxes act as the means for the regeneration of the human being. This is by inducing the rebuilding of cell membranes, which is essential for life. In the prevention of major diseases, such as viral syndromes, diabetes, fungal infestation, heart disease, arthritis, neurological syndromes, and cancer, this sterol and steroid nutrition to the cell wall is crucial. The establishment of healthy cell walls rich in sterols and steroids is perhaps the most critical element for the creation of vital health and, therefore, the resistance against degenerative diseases.

All degenerative diseases are associated with a deficiency of essential sterols and steroids. This is easy to prove. In a large percentage of people with degenerative conditions, such as cancer, diabetes, heart disease, lung disease, hypertension, and arthritis, there are obvious deficiencies, which are virtually routine. These are deficiencies of vitamin D, B complex, progesterone, cortisol, aldosterone, testosterone, certain forms of estrogens, and DHEA. All such substances are steroids. In particular, a low level of DHEA is a marker of premature aging and even premature death. It also tells of collapse of the body's coping mechanism—the adrenal glands. It means the body is consuming sterols/steroids faster than they can be replaced. Yet, DHEA is exclusively a steroid, a substance belonging to that category of foods that people with the aforementioned diseases so assiduously avoid. Chaga mushroom extracts provide the precursors to this life-enhancing steroid. Another important supplement is undiluted royal jelly (3x, fortified with wild rosemary and sage).

As mentioned previously chaga is the top source of SOD. In terms of protection against oxygen toxicity this enzyme is of even greater importance than the steroids/sterols. In natural emulsions the SOD is rendered absorbable so its function is maximized. In contrast, the extensive use of heat and noxious solvents disrupt the activity of this key substance, essentially rendering the enzymes inactive.

Chapter Two

Other Forest Cures

Tree bark and other forest cures have been used by the human race for countless centuries. One of the most potent tree barks is birch bark, which is discussed in later chapters. Other potent barks, as well as wild fruit found in or near forests, will be discussed in this chapter.

The power of the larch tree bark: medicinal bark and more

The larch tree, of the species *Larix laricina,* is one of the most profound blessings to humankind. Also known as the tamarack tree the bark, buds, and needles of this plant are completely edible. Moreover, they have been used as food and medicine for countless centuries. For instance, Native Americans used gum made from larch bark to ease upset stomachs. As well, the bark, which they consume as a tea, was relied upon to actually regenerate people who fell ill from diseases unknown. The needles are exceedingly high in vitamin C. A tea of these needles was used by both natives and settlers to cure symptoms of vitamin C deficiency.

The actual larch tree bark—or tamarack tree bark—is a potent forest cure. This bark was a major natural medicine of native tribes. As documented by James Duke in his book *Handbook of Northeastern Indian Medicinal Plants* are vast. Natives from a variety of regions used the bark infusion for persistant cough, gum disease, burns, ulcerations, tuberculosis, gonorrhea, chronic fatigue, muscle weakness, kidney disorders, congestive heart failure, weak heart, headaches, inflammation, and swelling. Research documents the basis of this use. ORAC testing has determined that the pulverized inner bark of this tree as a hot tea (available as Lovely Larch Tea) has an ORAC value of some 150,000 per 100 grams. Plus, it is a dense source of vitamin C, containing nearly 25 mg per 100 grams. Thus, it is one of the most potent natural medicines known.

Larch tree bark extract has significant biological actions. There are a number of studies demonstrating antitumor powers. Other studies, for instance, the work of Spoor, published in the *Canadian Journal of Physiology and Pharmacology*, show insulin-like actions. In the article, published in August 2001, tamarack was deemed "anti-diabetic." This is highly significant. The larch tree bark extract actually caused glucose to be driven into cells. Thus, there was an increase in the intracellular production of triglycerides. This is a good result, in other words, the fat was being produced where it should be— inside the cells, so it can be burned as fuel instead of in the blood where it wreaks havoc.

The potency of this forest cure is profound and diverse. Owen and Johns demonstrated in the *Journal of Ethnopharmacology* an action against gout. Here, it was determined, larch/tamarack bark extract directly inhibited the enzyme xanthine oxidase. Moreover, of 26 species of plants the larch bark extract was highest in inhibitory power at some 87%. Xanthine oxidase is the enzyme responsible for making uric acid, which may lead to the formation of urate crystals. It is these crystals, when deposited in the joints and muscles, which lead to gout attacks. Extract of larch tree bark blocks this.

Regarding the antitumor effects this is well documented. In *Chemistry and Pharmacology Bulletin* investigators in Tokyo found that the extract had a good effect against various cancer cell lines but exerted a particularly potent, specific action against colon cancer cell lines. Belgian investigators deemed the anticancer effects of the bark extract so potent that they regarded it as a "potential new anticancer" agent.

Larch bark is a dense source of nutrients. It contains a considerable amount of minerals and B vitamins. Moreover, in particular it is exceedingly rich in vitamin C. In the bark alone there is some 25 to 40 mg per 100 grams of this vitamin. Thus, as an emergency food in the wild this is invaluable. The bark is also rich in a wide range of plant chemicals with extensive medicinal properties. The various medicinal plant chemicals in larch bark include terpenes, diterpenes, phenolic compounds, including vanillic acid, *p*-coumaric acid, *p*-hydroxybenzoic acid, polyphenols, flavonoids, and a unique compound known as arabinogalactan. The latter is a kind of fibrous substance that is, in fact, an excellent source of dietary fiber. Yet, more than a mere fiber component it is one of the most medicinally active compounds in nature known.

Arabinogalactan is not only a fiber, but it is also a pre-biotic. This means that it is a key fuel which feeds the growth of healthy intestinal bacteria. These bacteria are, furthermore, essential to life. According to *Alternative Medicine Review*, 2000, arabinogalactan has been shown to cause an increase in production of intestinal butyrate. This substance acts as the preferred substrate for the production of energy by colon cells. This is crucial, because as long as these cells produce energy they remain healthy. When they lose their capacity to do so, it is then when they become diseased. *The Review* also noted the following finding, which was that arabinogalactan is vigorously fermented in the colon, causing an increase in the production of the highly beneficial bacteria bifidobacteria and lactobacillus. This may account for the discovery by American settlers that larch bark tea helps reverse intestinal disorders and/or the finding by the natives that arabinogalactan-rich tamarack bark is a generalized tonic for good health.

The compound was found to cause yet another beneficial effect in the intestinal canal. This is an action against ammonia, a chemical which can accumulate in the colon and blood as a consequence of liver and stomach disorders. It was found that arabinogalactan, when added to human fecal homogenates, caused a decrease in ammonia production.

The larch compound surely stimulates the colon and healthy bacteria cells, but it is also a general stimulant. By stimulant is meant the means for regeneration of health. Moreover, any substance which improves colon health will have a positive impact on the entire body. Thus, it has also been determined that arabinogalactan stimulates the production of key immune cells known as natural killer cells. In particular, regarding liver cancer cells larch tree extract was found to cause natural killer cell toxicity directed against such cells, primarily due to the stimulation of the release of gamma interferon. With the consumption of larch in the form of a tea made from the pulverized bark there is a general immune-enhancing action. There is also a general benefit to the heart and circulation. This may explain the high regard held by the natives for this plant, since they deemed the bark extract a universal medicine. Some tribes regarded it so highly that they proclaimed for the reversal of illness no other medicine is needed. Moreover, it is the larch bark infusion which they deemed useful for reversing weakness—and it's a weakness of constitution which is the modern plague. It is a most lovely, aromatic experience to drink this tea. Without doubt, it creates a sense of wellness and does so rapidly.

The sumac tree: edible and medicinal

When people see the word sumac, they often are concerned, thinking of the bush poison sumac. Yet, there are other types of sumac plants, which are completely different than the poisonous type. These are the so-called staghorn and smooth sumac plants. Rather than mere bushes these are actual trees or, perhaps, tall shrubs, which may grow as high as fifteen feet. On top of these shrubs are growths of clusters of berries, which were much relished by the Native Americans as both food and medicine. Yet, all parts of this tree are medicinal: the roots, bark, leaves, and berries.

Let us look at some of the native uses. The leaves were brewed for their astringent properties to make a diarrhea-fighting tea. For congestive heart failure natives drank a brew from a combination of the leaves, bark, and berries. For gum disease and bleeding gums they consumed a concentrated tea from the powdered leaves.

There were other diseases, according to native registries, which responded to sumac therapy. A. R. Hutchens in *Indian Herbalogy of North America* lists a wide range of benefits, deeming its actions "appreciably reliable," especially for afflictions of the mucous membranes, such as irritated/sore throat, laryngitis, diarrhea, and urinary/bladder disorders. It is also effective in vaginal discharge, vaginal candidiasis, irritation of the rectum, including hemorrhoids, and even, says Hutchens, rectal bleeding. As well, Russians found it useful in the treatment of arthritis. Middle Easterners have determined sumac as a remedy for heart disease and stomach disorders. These benefits may be the result of the general antiinflammatory action of its flavonoids.

The power of this tart fruit against bleeding is significant and is largely due to its rich content of tannic acid, which is a potent astringent. Incredibly, homeopaths have used sumac extracts for the reversal of a wide range of hemorrhages, including bleeding from the kidney and gums as well as intestinal bleeding and nose bleeds. The anti-bleeding action may also be due to the rich content of vitamin C. In fact, as a food sumac is no minor substance. Notes A. T. Vitale in her book *Leaves: in Myth, Magic, & Medicine* sumac berries are nutritionally dense. Incredibly, they contain, she notes, four times more vitamin C per weight than lemons. Plus, this is wild-source vitamin C. Because of its rich content of organic acids—malic, gallic, and tannic acids—sumac is naturally sour. With the vitamin C and the sour acids it is the ideal base for making a delicious and highly nutritious lemonade. Regardless, this explains why this tree was once called the lemonade tree or vinegar tree.

One such lemonade is available, known as Sumanade (Americanwildfoods.com). This is a pink 'lemonade' made with sumac berries, no lemon, and raw honey instead of sugar. Sumanade contains naturally occurring vitamin C, organic acids, and potassium. Another form of sumac is the pulverized powder as a tea. Combined with pulverized wild citrus this tea is delicious and nutritious, either hot or cold. Yet, it can also be made by gathering the sumac wild and making a home brew.

The value of the regular intake of a sumac-based drink and/or the pulverized tea is confirmed by modern research. Consider its powers against heart disease. In this regard one area of pathology relates to the overgrowth of cells in the arterial walls. Such an overgrowth is known as an atheroma or, essentially, tumor of the arterial wall. One of the integral components of the development of such tumors, which are key to the origin of atherosclerosis or hardening of the arteries, is a kind of cell known as vascular smooth muscle.

When stimulated by a toxin, this type cell actually migrates to the lesion to induce tumor growth. Anything which blocks the migration of such cells is therapeutic. In other words, if the migration can be halted the progression of hardening of the arteries is stopped.

At Canada's prestigious McGill University a study was undertaken to test sumac's powers in this regard. Recall that in the Middle East it has been long known that sumac berries have a heart-protective action. In the study, conducted by H. Zargham and R. Zargham and published in the *McGill Journal of Medicine*, an extract of sumac was added to stimulated vascular smooth muscle cells. Incredibly, the sumac extract vigorously halted the migration, causing the investigators to conclude that this natural medicine possesses "potent...activity" in the prevention of hardening of the arteries. They also concluded that the protective effects may well be superior to those of wine. This is for two reasons, and one is the fact that with wine there is toxicity combined with benefit. For instance, they note, the alcohol component of wine is known to increase the risks for certain types of heart disease as well as esophageal cancer. There is no such toxicity with sumac. Moreover, the types of artery-enhancing compounds found in wine are known as non-hydrolysable tannins. This means they cannot be easily hydrolyzed. In other words, they cannot be broken down for easy digestion. In contrast, the types found in sumac are hydrolysable, meaning they are readily broken down for easy absorption.

There are other unique actions, again, which confirm the more ancient use. For instance, Native Americans deemed sumac useful against vaginitis, sore throat, and skin infections. In addition, the Micmac tribe used it to treat ear infections and cough. In the case of earaches the Micmac would simply drip an infusion of the berries into the ear. Regardless, all such conditions are caused largely by infections. Thus, from the traditional use, clearly, sumac is an antiseptic. Pakistani researchers confirmed such a power. Publishing in the *Journal of Food Microbiology* these researchers found that sumac extract in a small concentration, ranging from 5% to less than 1%, inhibited the growth of a wide range of germs, including staph, bacillus, listeria, proteus, and E. coli. The growth of all 12 germs tested, which are common food spoilage organisms, was blocked.

A more in-depth investigation was undertaken by Rayne and Mazza in *Nature Preceding* through their article *Biological Activities of Extracts of Sumac (Rhus spp.): a Review.* Here, it was determined, extract of sumac is active against virtually all types of germs, notably bacteria, viruses, yeasts, fungi, and molds. Of all species of sumac it was the North American type, specifically *Rhus glabra*, which proved to be most potent. The sumac showed inhibitory power against a wide range of species, including:

staph
strep
bacillus
klebsiella
E. coli
proteus
enterobacter
pseudomonas
typhus bacteria
mycobacter
aspergillus
candida
fusarium
micosporum
sacchromyces
trichophyton
trichoderma

Regarding viruses it was active against the flu virus, parainfluenza, respiratory syncytial virus, adenovirus, measles, and herpes viruses 1 and 2. The activity against the latter is thought to be due to the rich content of potent antiviral flavonoids. With the antiviral activity some of the most potent compounds were found in the sumac seed, specifically the coating of this seed. Thus, whole food extracts, where the entire fruit is used, such as the pulverized whole food tea and the pulverized, strained sumac lemonade, offer the maximum potency. Regardless, the germ-killing properties should be no surprise, since, traditionally, sumac extracts were used essentially as antibiotics. The natives used them to kill gonorrhea, syphilis, and amebas. They even used sumac berries to cure infectious gangrene.

Yet, note the authors the powers of this fruit/spice are far more diverse than mere germ-killing. Yes, sumac is antifungal, antiviral, and antibacterial—whether used topically or internally. However, what these investigators made clear is the fact that this is one of the most useful, versatile natural medicines known. They deem it also to be an effective agent for preventing excessive blood clotting, in other words, having the power to prevent excessive stickiness of the blood. This is through an action against the clotting factors fibrin and thrombin. In regard to the cardiovascular system its antiinflammatory properties are also significant and are likely related to its rich content of flavonoids. Here, it has been determined, sumac extract blocks the formation of noxious forms of oxygen, the so-called hydroxyl radicals, which readily damage the arterial walls. It is also anti-hyperglycemic, meaning it helps fight hypoglycemia, diabetes, and syndrome X. This means that it has a potent power to support the function of the liver and pancreas. The combined actions against diabetes/syndrome X plus the prevention of excessive blood clotting make this sour spice an essential natural remedy for the prevention and reversal of heart disease, hardening of the arteries, and diabetes.

In this regard sumac has a number of mechanisms of actions. Besides directly interfering with excessive blood clotting it also blocks the formation of those highly dangerous lesions of the arteries known as atheromas. These are essentially tumors of the arterial walls. This fruit contains compounds which calm down the aggression within the arterial walls that results from oxidative stress.

Clearly, sumac is also an antitumor agent, which has been demonstrated in a number of studies. In this regard it has a property known as "cytotoxicity," meaning that it can cause the death of unwanted cells, including tumor cells but also the cells of eczema and psoriasis.

Regarding the antitumor actions a study was undertaken, which showed a direct effect. Publishing in the ACS Symposium Seminar, Perchellet and his group evaluated the powers of sumac extracts on the skin of mice after they were injected with cancer-causing chemicals. The cancer-causing chemicals provoked the development of skin cancers. Sumac, notably the wild American type, blocked the development of the cancers highly efficiently. The effect was so astounding that the researchers were led to conclude that this wild fruit is "valuable to prevent and/or inhibit" tumor growth.

In addition, sumac is a potent antioxidant. In the *Journal of Food Chemistry*, 2006, Turkish investigators tested this fruit versus synthetic antioxidants. They found that sumac is a highly effective antioxidant, vigorously scavenging free radicals. The extracts tested, noted the investigators, possessed "strong antioxidant activity." The activity was attributed to the rich content of anthocyanins and "hydrolysable tannins," notably gallic, malic, and tannic acids. Besides the tannins sumac is rich in a number of exceedingly powerful flavonoids. These flavonoids include quercitin, butein, sulfurtin, and fustin. The combination of these flavonoids plus the tannins makes this fruit an antioxidant powerhouse, which is unmatched by any common fruit. Remember, wild, remote-source sumac has an ORAC value of nearly 30,000 per 100 grams. In contrast, the ORAC value of certain commonly promoted fruit, such as acai and blueberry, is considerably lower. For instance, acai is some 16,000 per 100 grams, and blueberry is about 4000 per 100 gram. While all such fruit are valuable and nutritious, clearly, as far as all known fruit, the so-called super-fruit, wild sumac is the categorical leader.

Any sumac supplement must be made with fruit harvested from remote regions. Regarding ORAC/antioxidant levels sumac from the far remote regions of North America scores the highest in value. For the edible type of sumac spice the Mediterranean offers high-quality, remote sources. For true remote-harvested North American sumac of high purity (*Rhus glabra*) consume the wild pulverized tea combined with wild, pulverized citrus and/or the wild, honey-sweetened sumac beverage (Sumanade).

Another source of whole food sumac is the wild oregano capsules, which are commonly available in health food stores. Known as OregaMax capsules these represent an ancient traditional formula, where wild oregano is combined with sumac, the latter in the form of *Rhus coriaria*. Both wild oregano and *Rhus coriaria* are potent antioxidants, with the wild oregano scoring among the most vigorous of all antioxidants. The extracted oil of oregano alone has an ORAC level of some 300,000 per 100 grams. While no claim is made for OregaMax in relation to diseases what is certain is that the combination of wild oregano plus sumac offers an ideal antioxidant potency. OregaMax, a proprietary blend of wild oregano whole herb plus whole crushed wild sumac, is commonly found in health food stores.

Sumac is also a powerful antagonist to heavy metals. This would be expected from its rich content of the so-called organic acids, that is gallic, malic, and tannic acids. All such acids are aggressive binders of noxious metals. For instance, the sumac acids vigorously bind iron, and the latter metal is involved in increasing the toxicity of oxygen. It is believe that this iron-binding effect may partly account for the positive effects of sumac versus both cancer and heart disease, as iron is a cofactor in both diseases. Metals which may be bound and removed from the body through sumac consumption include iron, copper, mercury, and lead.

Thus, clearly, sumac is essential for human health. No wonder in many Middle Eastern countries it is a staple. The same is true in Turkey and some parts of Bulgaria, where sumac bushes grow in the mountains. Yet, in North America as well sumac bushes are found. Even so, here, this fruit or, rather, spice has never become a staple. This has now been resolved through the intake of wild, remote-source sumac extract, either as the whole crushed fruit/spice made into a cool or hot beverage. Another novel sumac source is Sumanade or wild North American sumac 'lemonade,' which is available as a gently sweetened beverage exclusively on the website Americanwildfoods.com. The latter is sweetened with raw, wild honey and is a delicious, as well as nutritious, way to gain the benefits of wild North American sumac. Moreover, the benefits of such a wild drink are demonstrated by the following case history:

Ms. L. is a 65-year-old woman with a history of suddenly developing bladder and urinary discomfort, although, chronically, she has always had sluggish kidneys. The new symptoms were relentless and led to a most disconcerting symptom, which was incontinence. Medical testing failed to confirm the cause, yet the discomfort and incontinence remained. She began drinking Sumanade, about four ounces daily, along with a cup of sumac tea. Within a few hours she noticed a considerable improvement in her urine stream. Within 24 hours the incontinence and urinary discomfort disappeared, never again to return. However, she experienced one interesting side-effect, which was weight loss. As wild sumac is a natural diuretic Ms. L. was pleased to experience a 3-pound weight reduction in a mere 48 hours. The sumac extract, she noted, brought her kidneys back to a healthier function, and she remains symptom-free.

Rose hips: forest bush, major medicine

On the edge of the forests there is a considerable amount of growth. There are plants which favor the forest environment. One of these is the wild rose.

This rose plant is entirely different than the commercial varieties. It is delicate if not subtle. The flower is highly friable and quickly wilts, unless immediately immersed in water. Yet, unlike the commercial rose this flower is highly edible and delicious. It is also a good source of vitamin C.

However, the most highly regarded portion of wild rose plants is the fall production, which is the rose hips. These hips are a dense source of nutrients. In particular, they are a top source of vitamin C and polyphenols.

Yet, not all rose hips are the same. Depending on the region some wild rose hips are vulnerable to disease, being attacked by worms and fungi. The best wild rose hips come from the most distant reaches of the northern forests possible. Here, they are relatively free of disease and infestation. These remote-source far northern rose hips are more aromatic than the more southerly varieties. They are also richer in vitamin C than many southern species. This is because, here, the rose plant is highly challenged by the intensely cold temperatures, and it responds by making a denser quantity of protective nutrients, including vitamin C, B complex, calcium, trace minerals, flavonoids, and polyphenols. Far northern rose hips are so potent that the potency can be smelled and tasted.

Like the larch bark and sumac, the far northern rose hips are available as a pulverized tea. For ideal health a teaspoonful or more can be consumed daily. This will provide wild, natural source vitamin C, B vitamins, calcium, magnesium, copper, iron, beta carotene, vitamin E, vitamin K, flavonoids, and polyphenols. The color tells all. It should be a rich, bright orange or orange-red. There should also be an obvious floral, sweet aroma. This is the assurance of freshness and biochemical power.

There have been a number of studies demonstrating the positive action of this forest remedy. In Denmark rose hips extracts are traditionally used for good health and also for the treatment of arthritis. As reported on *BBS News* in a six-month trial on arthritic patients a rose hips extract was found to increase activity and reduce joint pain.

Also, in Denmark rose hip powder was evaluated versus a more well-known treatment for arthritis, which is glucosamine. The researchers, led by R. Christensen of Denmark's Parker Institute, found that rose hips are effective in easing the symptoms of arthritis, while, incredibly, glucosamine had no effect. Further studies, for instance, Kharazmi's work published in *Osteoarthritis and Cartilage*, 2008, determined the profound mechanisms of action of the rose hips powder, which is the reduction of inflammatory actions of white blood cells, known as decreased chemotaxis. There was also a reduction in the production of proteins made by the body which promote inflammation, for instance, in human subjects levels of the inflammation marker C-reactive protein were reduced.

In a quality rose hips product the entire fruit must be used. This is rare, since with most extracts the highly nutritious seeds are ejected. Not so with the pulverized whole food tea. Here, the entire rose hip is pulverized—and, moreover, this is in a raw state, so all the nutrients are fully intact. According to T. S. Owen in her article "Benefit of

Rose Hips" the seeds must always be included in a quality rose hip tea. These seeds contain an oil which is highly beneficial to the internal organs and, particularly, the skin. In this oil is a potent form of vitamin A, known as trans retinoic acid, which is used in medicine to treat age-related damage to the skin such as age spots, sun-induced damage, hyperpigmentation, and wrinkles.

A thorough investigation was done on the various actions of the components of the rose hip seed. Doctors in Peru, led by B. Pareja and H. Kehl, actually applied oil of rose hip seeds to the skin of hundreds of patients. In one of the studies the oil was applied to surgical scars after the sutures were removed. Noted the investigators, "After three months of applying twice daily...it was noted that the scars were less apparent, without lumps and that skin elasticity had improved..." They also said that the typical surgical scars became "softer and less prominent" and that even acne scars, including the pits, were improved. One Chilean radiologist, Dr. H. Harbst, said that the rose hip oil application even helped loosen up fibrosis in the tissues. Any excessive pigmentation was curtailed, as was the typical bulking up of tissue (hypertrophy) about the scars. This led this physician to conclude that as a result of the rose hip treatment there is nearly a complete cure of the scars. The Peruvian doctors added to these results by finding that the oil reversed sun-induced skin damage, that is photo-aging, actually causing a virtually complete reversal of wrinkles and age spots. This effect was the result of its daily application. These effects may be largely due to the content in rose hip oil of naturally occurring vitamin A, and this is one of the few vegetable sources to contain it.

The consumption of vitamin C is also more rare than most people realize. Essentially, little is consumed in the modern diet. This is because food is rarely if ever consumed fresh, and losses of vitamin C after picking are continuous. Plus, virtually no one picks fresh, wild food and then immediately eats it, as was done by the ancestors. Furthermore, in modern society there are a number of stressors and/or toxins, which destroy the vitamin. So, people readily become depleted in vitamin C. This is why natural concentrates, such as wild rose hips and sumac, are so essential. They are true whole food supplements which must be added to the diet. These whole food supplements contain vitamins, minerals, fatty acids, flavonoids, polyphenols, and amino acids. By far the most dense source of vitamin C is wild camu camu, followed by acerola and rose hips.

The vitamin is essential for the structure of the bones, joints, muscles, and teeth. It is also needed for the repair of these organ systems. Furthermore, it helps maintain neurotransmitter function and also the function of the heart and arteries. Regarding the immune system vitamin C is essential and is needed for the normal function of all white blood cells.

Test yourself: are your symptoms due to vitamin C deficiency?

A deficiency of vitamin C is often subtle. Scurvy is gross deficiency, which is a kind of pre-death-like state. So, there are many more moderate forms of the deficiency. Take the following test to determine any degree of vitamin C deficit. Each response is worth one point unless otherwise noted.

Add up your score. Which of these apply to you?

1. weakness
2. muscle weakness
3. depression
4. feel exhausted easily
5. easy bruising (2 points)
6. nose bleeds (2 points)

7. blood vessels burst easily (2 points)
8. varicose veins (2 points)
9. spider veins (2 points)
10. popped veins/spider veins around the ankle (3 points)
11. hemorrhoids and/or rectal bleeding (2 points)
12. smoke on a daily basis (2 points)
13. smoke more a half pack to one pack daily (add 3 more points)
14. smoke one to two packs daily (add 3 more points)
15. smoke more than two packs daily (add 4 more points)
16. exposed regularly to second-hand smoke (2 points)
17. regularly work around chemicals
18. drink alcohol on a daily basis (2 points)
19. smoke cigars or pipes regularly (2 points)
20. rarely eat fresh fruit (3 points)
21. avoid the consumption of citrus fruit (3 points)
22. eat fresh dark greens only rarely (2 points)
23. swollen gums (2 points)
24. bleeding gums (3 points)
25. vague joint aches
26. stiffness of the joints and/or arthritis
27. aching in the bones or teeth
28. poor wound healing
29. irritability
30. bursitis-like pain
31. highly susceptible to colds/flu
32. petechiae (tiny hemorrhages due to capillary bleeding under the skin-3 points)
33. chronic anemia
34. visible hemorrhages under the skin (4 points)
35. take aspirin regularly (2 points)
36. take other antiinflammatory drugs regularly (2 points)
37. thinning of the skin or excessive skin aging
38. joints get stiff in cold weather
39. cold weather stresses the body

40. dryness of the mouth
41. listlessness and/or lethargy
42. hardening of the arteries (2 points)
43. chronic heart disease (2 points)
44. under a high amount of stress (2 points)
45. drink several cups of coffee daily
46. eat sweets regularly or use pure white sugar in drinks or food
47. take diuretics on a daily basis
48. intolerant to hot weather (heat exhaustion/heat stroke)
49. chronic headaches
50. pale complexion and pale lips
51. loose teeth
52. eat mostly cooked food (70% or more)

Your score_____

1 to 5 points: possible mild vitamin C deficiency
6 to 11 points: moderate vitamin C deficiency
12 to 17 points: severe vitamin C deficiency
18 to 23 points: extreme vitamin C deficiency
24 to 28 points: profoundly extreme vitamin C deficiency
29 and above: scurvy or pre-scurvy

In any score above 5 it is crucial to increase the consumption of natural-source vitamin C. The top food sources are citrus fruit, strawberries, papaya, mango, kiwi, guava, broccoli, Brussels sprouts, spinach, and dark green leafy vegetables. Food concentrates which offer invaluable amounts of the vitamin include wild, raw camu camu powder and wild pulverized rose hips, taken as a hot or cold beverage. Other top supplement concentrates include wild, raw sumac, acerola cherry, and red sour grape. For those in the severe, extreme, and profoundly extreme categories the daily consumption of pulverized northern-source rose hip tea, remote-source sumac tea, wild, raw strawberry juice, and wild, raw camu camu extract is highly advised. By far the most dense source is camu camu, which contains some 50 times more vitamin C per weight than oranges.

A true whole food plus vitamin C

Virtually all the nutrients that the body needs are found in the rose hip. I have always relished these God-given fruit in the wild, eating them right from the bush. From Americanwildfoods.com the wild, raw rosehips paste can be purchased and added to whole, non-homogenized milk, fruit smoothies, and even poured over stir-fry. Daily, I consume the wild, raw pulverized remote-source rose hip tea, either in hot or cold water. In hot water it creates a delicious infusion, but it is also tasty raw blended into cold water. I have yet to use rose hip oil but plan to begin doing so soon. Even so, by consuming the whole pulverized tea and the wild, raw concentrate the benefits of the oil are gained through internal consumption, since the oil components are found in these types, especially the pulverized tea. It is truly phenomenal to have sound health—to be strong and vital, like a wild creature. However, it is also astounding to see these benefits translated in human beauty—and it is guaranteed that if people regularly make use of extracts of wild, raw roses and their hips, there will be an improvement in appearance, just as has been documented by South American researchers.

People don't realize the degree of vitamin C deficiency which they suffer. Moreover, a lack of this nutrient negatively affects all organ systems. The vitamin is water soluble, which means it is not well retained. Furthermore, under stress it is readily depleted. This surely includes psychic stress, but it also includes physical stress, particularly the stress of harsh weather. In this regard I have my own case history which is significant. The weather in Chicago was extremely cold with a wind chill of about zero degrees. Myself and my wife were out all day shopping and doing odd chores; the cold apparently had an impact. The next day neither of us was functional. Plus, in both cases our joints were stiff. I reasoned this was due to vitamin C depletion and that such depletion negatively affects the adrenals, causing inability to function. I made a combination drink of the pulverized wild sumac plus the vitamin C-rich and delicious remote-source pulverized rose hips. In a blender in a quart or so of water I added a large heaping tablespoon of both powders and whipped this, along with two tablespoons of wild oregano honey. Then, each of us drank this.

The result was astounding. We were fully functional the rest of the day and full of energy. Despite the fact that it was about zero degrees also that day I went out for a one-mile walk and tolerated it fully. This shows the great power of wild, raw remote-source vitamin C extracts, the kind of extracts that give people the power to function, regardless of the stress or issue. I followed this with a daily dose of wild camu camu capsules, along with the aromatic 'lovely' Larch tea, with stupendous results and much resilience against the cold.

As everyone knows synthetic vitamin C cannot do this. Only raw nature has the power to regenerate people—to bring them better health. This is surely true of vitamin C, which only has its nutritional and disease-prevention powers when it is extracted from nature.

Actually, today, synthetic vitamin C is toxic. This relates to the raw material, which is corn sugar. This corn sugar is derived from genetically engineered corn. Scientific studies have demonstrated that this type of corn is noxious. This may explain common complaints from people who take synthetic vitamin C supplements such as bloating, indigestion, burning sensations, and irritable bowel.

Essentially, the body is rejecting this artificial vitamin C. Thus, the consumption of the synthetic is not only a waste of money but is also destructive. The regular consumption of synthetic vitamin C is associated not merely with digestive disruption but, incredibly, also with an increase in sudden death and for pregnant women birth defects.

This dilemma is easy to solve. A person must simply switch from such artificial forms to whole food sources. Surely, this includes increasing the consumption of the top food sources such as citrus fruit, kiwi, papaya, strawberries, broccoli, spinach, Brussels sprouts, and dark leafy greens. Yet, it also demands the regular use of food concentrates, especially those made from wild remote-source fruit such as wild camu camu concentrates, pulverized sumac, and pulverized aromatic rose hips. Moreover, ideally for maximum potency and effect all such concentrates/powders must be raw.

This is the basis of life, this intake of fresh, live food. Then, too, any live food is at least a good source of vitamin C. Even live raw meat, as well as raw milk, has at least a life-sustaining amount of the vitamin. In this live form vitamin C is necessary for survival. This was demonstrated by early research by the British investigator Robert McCarrison. Notes C. Scott in his book *Health, Diet, and Common Sense* the studies of McCarrison demonstrated a crucial fact. This was in relation to the consequences of a lack of vitamin C in the food. In studying rats, some 2300 of them, this investigator determined that with a diet of cooked food there was profound damage. All the test animals on a solely cooked food diet degenerated. This was true even though this diet contained some foods which are normally a good source of vitamin C, but, again, they were in a cooked form. As demonstrated in Scott's book, incredibly, all the organs of these vitamin C-deficient animals were damaged. This is why it is reasonable to state that for any chronic disease the daily intake of crude whole food vitamin C sources is a boon and will likely quickly lead to an improvement. For such whole food sources see Americanwildfoods.com. Here, the top sources of the vitamin are wild, raw camu camu, wild, raw rose hips paste, wild, raw strawberry extract and wild, raw pulverized rose hips powder.

Thus, within and on the edges of forests there are a wide range of cures. One of these is found on the edges of the Amazon River. This is the wild camu camu, the richest source of vitamin C known.

The powers of camu camu: vitamin C and more

On the edges of the Amazon River grows a bush of vast importance. The bush, known as camu camu, bears a fruit which is most unusual. This is because this fruit contains as much as three percent vitamin C by weight.

The camu camu plant, which is actually a shrub growing up to eight feet high, hangs over the edges of rivers and lakes. The main consumer of the fruit are fish, as the camu camu berries drop into the water for their consumption. The color of the outside of the fruit varies from red to purple.

Brazilian, as well as Peruvian, investigators have done a thorough analysis of this fruit. It is "extremely sour," which is due to the inordinately high vitamin C content, 'much higher than acerola or citrus juice.' These investigators found that the peel has a massive amount of vitamin C, some 5% by weight. They also found that the maximum vitamin content is established in the ripe fruit, when it turns deep orange-red color. This sun-ripened wild type, which is hand harvested by the natives, is the ideal form to consume supplementally. Plus, by buying this type this supports the local indigenous people, whose livelihood is dependent upon nature.

One such supplement is available. A purely wild camu camu-based vitamin C supplement, it is enriched with acerola, red sour grape, rose hips, and *Rhus coriaria*. All these are wild and/or remote-source concentrates. Look for such a diverse formula made with exclusively wild-source camu camu, picked at the height of ripeness, along with the aforementioned ingredients, at high quality health food stores. Such a formula is a dense source not only of wild-source vitamin C but also minerals and flavonoids.

Camu camu, rhus, and sour grape contain a number of properties in addition to their vitamin C density. All such fruit are natural preservatives. As mentioned previously rhus is a potent antioxidant. In particular, the preservative properties of this fruit, along with red sour grape, are exceptionally potent. In this regard both camu camu and rose hips powders tend to oxidize readily, and thus the vitamin C losses over time can be significant. Thus, such a combination is ideal, because, due to the preservative powers of the ingredients, the vitamin C remains fresh and the potency remains intact. Of note, as published by Brazilian researchers there is over a year's time as much as a 30% loss in vitamin C levels in camu camu that is not preserved. Thus, by adding the potent antioxidant preservatives red sour grape and *Rhus coriaria* the vitamin C content of the purely natural vitamin C supplement is preserved.

The purely natural vitamin C supplement contains some 150 mg of the wild-source vitamin per two capsules. This amounts to 250% of the minimum daily requirement, which is significant. Thus, for mild vitamin C deficiency one capsule daily of such a vitamin C complex is sufficient. For moderate deficiency two or more capsules per day is ideal. Regarding severe deficiency three to four capsules daily must be consumed, while for extreme and profoundly extreme states the consumption should be at least three capsules twice daily. For those with pre-scurvy or scurvy the consumption should be three capsules four times daily. This is also available as a bulk powder, which may be taken in equivalent doses. With vitamin C higher doses are likely to create improvement at an accelerated rate, since this vitamin is quickly depleted from the body and is essential for life processes. The richer the blood levels are that can be maintained the greater will be the degree of health improvement and prevention. Other supplemental sources of vitamin C, which can be taken on a daily basis to support the camu camu therapy, include wild, raw rose hips paste and raw remote-source strawberry extract (available on Americanwildfoods.com), along with pulverized wild, raw rose hips and sumac.

Thus, besides trees and their growths there are a wide number of other forest cures which are worthy of study. This book covers only a modicum of these. Yet, chaga is surely one of the most potent of all forest medicines. However, the greatest advantage is reaped by the consumption of a wide variety of such cures. Taken together, rose hips, sumac, camu camu, and chaga are an excellent combination. Pulverized rose hips tea is also a potent source of polyphenols and, thus, scores high on the ORAC scale. There is also the wild, raw poplar bud emulsion, as well as pulverized wild birch bark. Pulverized larch (tamarack) tree bark is another ideal natural medicine for rapid improvement and, ultimately, powerful health. All such wild complexes are edible whole foods of an exceedingly high nutritional density. These are ideal whole food supplements to add to the diet for optimal health. They are also ideal for the prevention of disease and therefore the extension of lifespan. The body needs the nutrients found in forest cures for ideal health. Yet, of all forest cures which were studied in the creation of this book chaga proved to be the most versatile. This is because it contains the broadest complement of nutrients and phytochemicals. Now, let us reveal more about chaga mushroom, the king of all plants.

Chapter Three

Wild Nature: Proving Ground

There are no powers comparable to the powers of wild nature. In the wild there is a great deal of strain on plants. This stress forces them to produce great medicines. The greater the degree of stress the more powerful are the medicines which are created. Then, such medicines can be harvested for human use. It is strictly wild plants that have sufficient medicinal powers to act as cures. Farm-raised plants have far less curative properties. This includes even organic plants, which, while healthy, are not nearly as potent as wild ones. In the wild plants are challenged by every conceivable stress, including the extremes of weather, elevation, harsh surroundings, pathogens, and insects. Thus, such plants produce a plethora of biological compounds in their defense. When humans ingest such wild plants, they gain the benefit of these protective chemicals. This is the basis of the cures mentioned in this book.

Harsh climate, powerful cures

To appreciate chaga mushroom's medicinal powers a person must understand the nature of birch trees and their growths.

These living entities survive among the harshest climactic conditions on this earth. They have the power to survive winters of the most extreme degree, with temperatures as low as -70 degrees Centigrade. Rather, the birch and poplar trees, as well as their mushrooms, thrive in such conditions. Chaga itself is only produced by trees existing in the 45th Parallel and above, in other words, it is a cold-stress fungus. So, what is in such living entities which allows for their survival? It is the potent sterols which are largely responsible. Just like wax protects the outer parts of a car from weather-related damage so do the sterols protect the northerly trees from the extremes they endure. Without these waxes the trees would die.

Human beings can take advantage of this. The chaga and tree bark extracts are top sources of these waxes in the form of biologically active sterols such as inotodiol, betulin, and betulinic acid. Again, the active ingredients are used by the trees for survival as well as strength. Thus, for a person suffering from poor stamina or exhaustion extracts of birch bark and/or chaga mushroom are highly beneficial. The same is true for those suffering from a failure to thrive such as children who are not developing properly or people with muscle wasting diseases. As well, those with weak organs, particularly weak lungs, muscles, heart, and kidneys, will benefit vastly. In all such cases the chaga and bark extracts are the ideal nutritional supplements to consume.

It must be reiterated: the physical strength of all cells is dependent upon sterols/steroids. Yet, it is not merely the structural needs of the cells and major organs, which the tree medicines rectify. Failure of function, which leads to poor development, poor energy, and physical degeneration, is essentially failure to cope. In particular, extracts of chaga mushroom are crucial for reversing this, because this mushroom increases the body's ability to cope with the various stresses it must endure. For instance, this endocrine function, that is the function of the hormone system, is responsible for the human's ability to cope—and through their rich content of sterols chaga, as well as birch bark, feed this. As a nutritional source of sterols chaga and birch bark reign supreme. Remember, chaga routinely endures weather that would kill a human in a matter of days or, rather, hours. So, it is no surprise that in virtually every way chaga mushroom and birch bark extracts support the body's stress resistance capacity. Anyone can realize this by taking them. Virtually immediately there will be an increase in strength, energy, and stress tolerance. All these are signs that chaga and birch bark extracts, rich in biologically-active sterols, rapidly cause the body to achieve balance. To reiterate the best sterol-rich tree supplements are emulsified extract of white birch bark, emulsified extract of wild, raw chaga mushroom, and chaga mushroom-birch bark tea (or expresso). For optimal results all three should be taken.

This can be supported by the intake of extract of poplar buds. The buds of poplar offer medicinal properties different from the birch bark medicines. This is because these buds are rich in phenolic acids. The phenolic acids are potent antiseptics. They are also exceedingly powerful antiinflammatory agents. One of these phenolic acids is the pain-relieving chemical salicin, the same active ingredient in aspirin. For instance, for structural disorders, pain syndromes, joint swellings, nerve injuries, brain injuries, and diseases of inflammation the combination of poplar bud extract with chaga mushroom emulsion is powerful medicine. Another forest cure to use for such syndromes is wild, raw multiple berries extract, as drops under the tongue.

Rare and wild: gift from nature?

Chaga mushroom doesn't merely grow everywhere. It cannot be found on birch trees, for instance, growing in warm climates. Even in regions of moderately cold winters, such as the midwest of America or middle Europe, it doesn't exist. Thus, this is a rare natural medicine, which must be savored. In this respect chaga mushroom extracts are to be respected and recognized as a blessing, particularly for the much overburdened humankind with its litany of diseases.

Both chaga and birch bark extracts are potent agents for the reversal of human diseases. Here, where there is little hope, where there is nothing but degeneration and pain, chaga and birch bark offer much hope. These are particularly powerful for the cure of disorders related to the immune system, that is where this system is impaired. They also create a vitality in human beings that they never before experienced. Thus, they truly are medicines of youthfulness.

A person must respect this immense power. It is rare to have a nutritional supplement which offers such diverse actions. What's more, surely, the mushroom itself is a rare production. Thus, every bit of it must be cherished. Too, as the demand increases there must be care not to cause needless damage to the environment. For instance, birch bark must ideally be harvested from freshly downed trees or trees cut for lumber. This is the type of bark that was used by the original researchers, who showed the bark extract's anticancer effects. There is no need to damage living trees. The birch bark used in the chaga infusion/expresso, as well as the spice oil emulsion, is utilized from such sources. Regarding chaga the key here is to harvest primarily the large growths. These growths occur on dying birch trees. Thus, in this case when the chaga is harvested, there is no major damage to the environment, because the life of the tree has essentially ended.

There is another concern, which is the fact that there are artificially produced forms of this mushroom being produced. The issue here is safety as well as efficacy. Wild chaga is entirely safe for human consumption. It is this type which has been used historically and which has been demonstrated effective for the improvement of health. For this reason only the truly wild type should be consumed.

Cultured chaga produced in vats cannot be relied upon as a cure, because this is unnatural. There is no way true this wild mushroom can grow in this environment. This is a violation of nature, because chaga is strictly a product of extremes, and it is such extremes which cause it to produce its potency. The extremes of nature keep the mushroom free of dangerous microbes. Yet, in contrast, in a man-made environment potentially dangerous microbes and other contaminants are serious risks. Plus, the synthetic product is far weaker and, in fact, different biochemically than the wild type. Without the challenge of fighting against the harshness of nature the chaga is rendered impotent.

It makes no sense to produce it this way. It doesn't grow inside buildings or in a laboratory. Nor does it grow in a commercial vat. Regardless, wild chaga, as a natural growth of birch trees, is time tested. For nearly 5000 years there are records of its use. It was even used before this time. This was through a man found frozen in time, the Ice Man of the Alps, found in a thawing glacier, who had in his possession a precious supply of chaga mushroom.

Asian experience

The Chinese deemed it "A Gift from God." Of the thousands of medicinal foods and herbs used by these people no other was given such a status. Why did the ancient Asians regard it so highly? It is because even in the earliest eras of human history the powers of this natural medicine were obvious. The ancient Chinese doctors determined that chaga was highly unusual, because it had the capacity to perform several functions at once. For instance, it purged the body of toxins and improved digestion, while also activating immune function. They also observed, clearly, that its regular intake increased lifespan. Chaga, the Chinese determined, achieves what no other substance in their pharmacy could ever achieve, which is to keep people healthy by keeping them free of deadly diseases. This is confirmed in the original oriental medical almanac, *Shen Nong Ben Cao Jing*, where chaga is classified as a medicinal herb of the highest class. Yet, this is true only of the naturally found or wild mushroom. It is this which is the truly divine gift. Thus, a person should be sure that any chaga extracts which are consumed are purely wild and are not fabricated.

Today, in the East, that is Asia, chaga is in wide use. Here, people consume it for a litany of health issues, including cancer, heart disease, arthritis, chronic fatigue, and high blood pressure. More commonly, they take it for general health such as to strengthen the immune system, increase vitality, and improve skin health. Chaga and similar natural medicines, which are there in vogue, have much to do with the increasing vigor of the Asian civilization. In contrast, in most arenas Western peoples lack such vigor. This is especially true in the work-place. Perhaps if Americans used natural medicine habitually, as is done in the Orient, and, therefore, took full advantage of nature's gifts, perhaps then they could again compete. Yet, there is another factor that is necessary. This is the halting of the excess use of pharmaceutical agents, which instead of extending lifespan shorten it. Americans and Europeans are the primary consumers of such drugs. Thus, the degeneration of American and European civilization is due in part to the degeneration in peoples' health, largely at the hands of pharmaceutical houses. Through a reliance on nature Asians are attempting to stall this degeneration. Western people would be well advised to do the same. Yet, will Western people adopt the good habits to do so?

In primitive cultures all over the world people have taken certain actions to stay healthy. Such an approach has been lacking in modern society. This is largely because such society lacks any direct ties to tradition and, particularly, to the healing powers of nature. Also, nature was relied upon by the ancients, who had no pharmaceutical drugs. In those eras people had no option but self-care. In fact, such self-care was critical, because how could the early people deal with degenerative disease? They had no facilities for caring for the sick. To survive they had to stay well. Thus, they learned certain artifices to achieve this. One of these was the ingestion of preventive medicines such as chaga, raw honey, bee pollen, wild raw berries, medicinal roots, and similar sources of life-giving power.

Mountain tribes of Siberia had a tough life. Chaga was one of the substances they used to compensate for this. Some of these tribes consumed it every day. This was largely for general health, but they also used it as an emergency medicine in particular for respiratory disorders. Such disorders are a common cause of death in this region. By preventing sudden death from respiratory infection, such as pneumonia, tuberculosis, bronchitis, and the flu, there is a profound result. This causes a significant increase in lifespan. So, it is true, as a result of the routine ingestion of chaga and birch bark certain Siberian tribespeople lived to be in their late 90s and early 100s, which is unheard of for arctic people. The key is that those who enjoyed such longevity used the mushroom regularly. The same pattern has been seen in Canadian aborigines, who are regular consumers of this invaluable medicine.

With time it became well known that in chaga consumers the health was extraordinary. In more modern times—the 1100s A.D.—the use of chaga became more mainstream, with even Russia's rulers depending upon it. One such ruler, Czar Vladimir Monamah, used it for treating his cancer. From central Russia its use spread eastward to the Baltic countries, where this mushroom also became famed as a health aid. Today, in eastern Europe chaga tea is a common domestic therapy for general health. The Japanese have also adopted the mushroom for health maintenance. Here, a significant amount of research has been published demonstrating chaga's significant powers in activating the immune system. In Japan this mushroom is deemed, appropriately, the "Diamond of the Forest." In fact, it is more valuable than any diamond—and much less stressful and toxic to find.

Gift from heaven

Chaga mushroom and birch bark have dramatic actions on the body. This is largely through the creation of cellular energy, which is greatly deficient in modern people. Then, this action is immediate. A person takes these natural medicines, and quickly he/she feels a lift. There is a clarity in thinking. There is a sense of calm, even peace. This is largely the result of the rich content of the highly rare superoxide dismutase as well as the exceptional content of biologically active sterols. These rare substances are immediately utilized by the body for key physiological processes, including the pumping of the heart, the production of adrenal steroids, vitamin D synthesis, and immune surveillance. The rich content of pantothenic acid in chaga is also highly valuable, since this vitamin boosts internal synthesis of steroids and SOD.

The sterols are a potent source of human nutrition. Biochemically, these are readily used by human cells. These molecules are a significant source of oxygen. So is SOD. There is also beta glucan, found in significant amounts in chaga, which increases the energetics of the immune system. In addition, sterols are used by the body to create hormones, and it is the hormones which are responsible for the production of cellular energy.

As mentioned previously sterols are also used for strengthening cell membranes. There are trillions of such membranes in the body, and they all need a daily supply of both sterols and steroids, including cholesterol. There is also the positive influence of sterols on heart function. These substances help reduce the thickness of the blood, thereby improving blood flow. They also act to prevent fatty deposits in the arteries. This is the opposite of what is taught. After all, the so-called good cholesterol that binds fats, HDL cholesterol, is still a sterol—and a kind of cholesterol at that. Yet, plant sterols have a unique action of blocking the excessive accumulation of animal cholesterol in the blood. No wonder the intake of sterol-rich chaga and birch bark extracts (chaga is also the top source of SOD) causes a virtual immediate increase in both strength and energy as well as an improvement in circulation. Moreover, it is not anyone's imagination. Rather, it is very real.

Is it really possible? Perfect health in minutes?

It may be difficult to believe, but there is a vast power in tree medicines for humans—and the benefits are virtually immediate. This is the creation of a kind of vitality that humans so desperately desire. It is also the creation of internal power, which is also rapidly achieved.

For most people the achievement of vital health remains elusive. The search for a simple cure is the real desire. People need simplicity in life, not more complications. No one wants to make the effort for health improvement arduous. Even so, it is rare for a substance to produce such powerful effects that they are virtually immediate. Chaga does this. So do extracts of birch bark and poplar buds. However, the effects of chaga are the most obvious and rapid. The chaga is taken, and, then, virtually immediately there is the clear result. This is an increase in power, stamina, and energy. Additionally, there is an increase in mental alertness. There is also a heightened resistance to disease, in fact, a kind of immunity against it. With the intake of this complex there is a kind of exceptional strength that develops. The person can more readily tolerate stress. The rich content of sterols and immune potentiators, such as beta glucan, give the body fighting power. As well, the desire for exercise increases, as does the tolerance for hard labor. A person who is athletic will notice enhancements—in speed, stamina, and strength. Weight lifters notice they can lift more aggressively and, perhaps, gain an increase in strength. This increase in strength can be as much as 20% or more. This increase in strength is demonstrated by the following case history:

> Mr. D is a 60-year-old man who has been a weight/power lifter for nearly 45 years. In all this time he tried numerous supplements but nothing made a noticeable difference—until he took the chaga as both the spice oil emulsion and the tea/expresso. Said Mr. D., because of those supplements, "I significantly increased my repetitions plus I am stronger." Additionally, after working out he said, "I experienced no soreness, so I felt like I didn't even work out, while normally I would be sore."

Competitive runners gain in endurance and, thus, achieve a decrease in running time. Even with mental tasks there is an increase in stamina. People needing high levels of mental powers—speakers, writers, authors, and journalists—notice significant enhancement of their capacities. As a result of the regular intake of chaga extracts or the hot beverage these people have seemingly continuous stamina to pursue their work. People who tire easily from sedentary efforts, like driving, mental tasks, and desk work, also respond greatly to chaga.

Non-athletic people benefit greatly. Here, a consequence occurs that some people might find truly bizarre. This is the desire to exercise, which is so overpowering that it must be fulfilled. This is the degree of energy that chaga extracts can create within the body. There are few if any substances on this earth that can produce such a wide range of effects so quickly and so potently. Its unusual powers in this regard are demonstrated by the following case history:

> Mr. V. is a 45-year-old production manager at a nutritional supplement company. He takes numerous supplements but still had no desire to work after hours nor to do any strenuous exercising. He heard about the emulsified chaga mushroom extract (spice oil-enhanced) and so began taking it, about forty drops under the tongue.
>
> Without thinking that night he went home and vigorously mowed the lawn, for which he normally procrastinates. Then, in what was an unheard of event for this sedentary individual he organized a soccer game and played for several hours. "Never before," he said, "have I ever experienced such a surge of energy from a nutritional supplement."

For extra strength and energy the chaga emulsion can be taken every day. Regarding the energy needed for daily tasks the effect of chaga, particularly the emulsified extract as drops under the tongue, is immediate. Virtually any daily energy lag can be reversed by placing a few drops under the tongue and holding them for a few minutes before swallowing. This includes the typical mid-morning and mid-afternoon sluggishness. It also includes fatigue from driving, stress, mental exhaustion, or excessive exercise. All this is obliterated by using the wild, raw chaga extract, particularly as sublingual drops. The latter are conveniently used for quick results whenever a boost in energy is needed. This boost in energy is largely due to the sterol content, since these molecules exert potent hormone-like effects on the body. It is also the result of the intake of chaga's various oxygen-rich compounds, particularly superoxide dismutase. The point is whenever a person needs an energy boost this wild mushroom should be consumed. This was the main reason it was consumed by the primitives. For many diseases the results are essentially immediate. As a consequence of the daily intake of the chaga and/or birch bark extracts people notice that, systematically, many of their conditions are resolved. Stomach disruptions, including gastritis and ulcers, are reversed, cancers are methodically destroyed, diabetic conditions are eliminated, musculoskeletal pain is systematically eased, high blood pressure is lowered, and inflammatory skin disorders are cured. Chaga and birch bark extracts are among the few natural substances that have such diverse, positive effects on such a wide range of conditions. This is why even to this day in eastern Europe and parts of Russia chaga and birch bark are regarded as universal medicines.

For centuries the Russians have relied upon chaga for health maintenance. Its intake, they know, is essential for the creation of daily power. Russians and Siberians report that they notice the difference from the intake of chaga virtually immediately—and also are cognizant of what happens to them when they fail to take it, that is they are not nearly so energetic. There are few if any other natural substances that offer such immediate power.

Now, all people could use an immediate boost. Like the Russians and Siberians, they can achieve this with just the daily intake of chaga, ideally in the form of emulsified drops and a hot infusion, with added white birch bark and purple/black maca. Now, the secret behind the power of physically fit Russians is revealed. Also, it is now known why Russian power-lifters and wrestlers were virtually invincible. It is the SOD- and sterol-rich chaga that is more greatly responsible for their physical prowess, as well as longevity, than any other food/substance.

The extracts: capturing the power of forest cures

The cure may be in the forest. However, the question is how can this curative power be captured for human use? When fresh with the full potency intact, these forest medicines are exceptional. This is proven by the health of the creatures which rely on them such as bear, moose, deer, elk, martin, mink, song-birds, wild turkey and grouse. None of these animals suffer from the terminal diseases so common in humans such as heart disease, diabetes, arthritis, and/or cancer. Obviously, this is the result of their wild food-based diet.

This proves that the divine-source food is a cure. In other words, the natural unaltered productions have precisely what the beings in this earth need for survival as well as maintaining optimal health. This itself is a miracle. True it may not be easy to find these productions. It may take a greater amount of work to find these foods than any energy that is derived from them, in terms of calories. Yet, what is clear is that such foods can only enhance health, in other words, they could never cause disease. Rather, their intake is preventive, even curative. Wild food, such as wild chaga mushroom, wild birch bark, wild berries, and wild greens, block the development of major degenerative diseases such as cancer, heart disease, high blood pressure, arthritis, atherosclerosis, kidney disease, Parkinson's disease, Alzheimer's disease, multiple sclerosis, tuberculosis, and diabetes. This is partly because of the extraordinarily rich content of vitamins and minerals in such food, but it is also the result of their exceptional antioxidant powers. It is also due to the high density of flavonoids, far higher than that found in any farm-raised food.

Processed food, that is man-made food, is entirely different. Not only does it fail to block such diseases but, rather, it actually causes them. This is proven by the fact that when wild animals are fed a diet of such food, they rapidly succumb to human-like diseases. Yet, for the wild food to be exceptional—that is in the prevention of disease—it must be in the raw state. In this way it is medicinal. Cooked, it is healthy, but it may not be sufficiently potent to cure disease. Even so, hot infusions are more effective in curative powers than heat-treated extracts. When, for instance, a tea or herb is merely immersed in just-boiled water and allowed to steep, this is an acceptable method.

When in the raw state, the enzymes are intact, and these are medicines in their own right. This is why even with extracts of wild berries these must be raw. Even so, again, for many wild medicines which can be converted into a powder or tea another acceptable method is to use hot water as an extraction agent, where the just-boiled water is poured over the medicine. This is a time-tested method for making medicinal extracts, especially from roots, barks, and mushrooms. This method preserves the majority of medicinal compounds.

Like the animals humans can immunize themselves from the torment of degenerative disease by consuming natural cures. Yet, when combining tradition with science, there are ways to even improve upon nature. For instance, traditionally chaga mushroom has been used by itself. Yet, as described by Russian investigators "it is a scientific fact" that when chaga mushroom is combined with birch bark its therapeutic properties are enhanced. Notes one of the key chaga mushroom researchers, Gaiina Mikhaylovna, Chairman, Irkutsk State Medical University, the white part of this bark contains rich supplies of the active ingredients of chaga, notably betulin, betulinic acid, and lupeol. Then, when this bark is combined with the chaga there is great synergy. Note Russian pharmaceutical investigators, "The very compound that makes birch 'shine bright white' has been tentatively linked to (the) treatment for such devastating human ailments as…melanoma or cancer, several forms of herpes, and even AIDS." The Russians continue, saying, "Betulin, a powdery substance in the outer bark of the birch tree, has been shown to help wounds heal faster and cut inflammation." They also note that this substance has equal efficacy in the destruction of a variety of experimental tumors as any drug. Furthermore, their investigations show, birch bark extracts are entirely non-toxic, whether for humans or animals.

The ideal forest cure is to combine therapy with wild northern forest chaga mushroom and wild remote-source birch bark. This is found in a food supplement, where the chaga and birch bark, along with organic purple/black maca, are powdered. Then, this is consumed as a hot water infusion, that is a chaga/birch bark expresso. The chaga and birch bark plus maca are ground into a fine powder for use as a hot or cold beverage. Thus, in this state both these foods are raw. Then, water is boiled. The just boiled water may be allowed to set for a moment and then poured over this powder. This is allowed to steep for a few minutes and then drunk. Even so, the best method is to let this mixture sit for 24 to 48 hours, and then drink either hot or cold. The hot water acts as an extracting agent, increasing the absorption of the active ingredients. This is the traditional method. Apparently, as long as the chaga/birch bark is not boiled extensively in water there is no damage to the active ingredients, particularly the waxy sterols. Thus, a mere hot water soaking is sufficient to extract the medicinal power. This chaga/birch bark expresso or tea gives the greatest benefits if drunk daily. However, it is beneficial to drink it at least every other day. Even twice weekly is highly beneficial. The ancient—and long-lived—Siberians took it daily as a tea.

The hot water infusion is supplemented by a true raw extract, which is the emulsified wild chaga drops. Here, chaga is extracted as a fatty emulsion. The resulting cream-like chaga is taken as drops under the tongue. There is no birch bark in this emulsion, since the latter, when emulsified, is lumpy, whereas the pure emulsified chaga is creamy. The value of a fatty emulsion is proven by scientific studies, for instance, it was Mullauer publishing in *Experimental Oncology and Radiology* who demonstrated the connection. In this research it was found that the efficacy of chaga is significantly enhanced through the addition of cholesterol. In other words, through a fatty emulsion the components of chaga and, therefore, birch bark become more activated. This is because cholesterol is a key substance for the emulsification of fats. As mentioned previously this means the intake of fatty foods aids in the absorption of these active ingredients, as found in both chaga and birch bark.

The fatty emulsion is made through a specialized method of mixing chaga with aromatic bark and spice oils such as oils of cinnamon and clove. The result is the production of a highly potent extract of chaga mushroom, as drops under the tongue. Through this process the full power of this mushroom is captured as well as utilized. The emulsification process liberates the sterols, that is the waxes and lipids, from the chaga membranes, rendering them absorbable. Thus, the extract can merely be placed under the tongue or consumed on an empty stomach or with food. Furthermore, this is a chemical-free solution, plus it is raw. Both the emulsified extract and the dried wild chaga/birch bark expresso are invaluable in the treatment of human disease.

There are other wild, raw extracts, which are highly medicinal. These include extracts of wild raw greens, wild raw berries, and various other barks, buds, and mushrooms. The therapeutic properties of such forest cures will be discussed throughout this book.

There is great power in nature. However, when harvesting medicines, much of this is lost in the processing. To maximize the power all effort should be made to capture the critical essences. Furthermore, any extraction/processing should be done in a natural, whole way. As proven by a number of scientific studies isolates are less effective than the whole. Additionally, extracts produced in a non-toxic way are more potent and safe than those produced with the use of chemicals such as hexane, methanol, and alcohol. Regarding the latter these disturb the molecular structure of natural compounds. Plus, these chemicals are toxic to the internal organs, especially the liver, kidneys, adrenal glands, bone marrow, and stomach lining. These toxins are also poisonous to the environment, which is another reason to shun solvent extracted herbs.

Some herbal extracts, for instance, contain as much as 60% alcohol, making them veritable drugs. In those with a weaker tolerance to this chemical this can greatly disrupt body function and can surely poison the liver. In contrast, whole food extraction agents, such as raw vinegar, extra virgin olive oil, hot water, steam, and spice oils, not only fail to disturb the molecular potency but also enhance it. Nor do they exhibit toxicity to organs, rather, they enhance them. All the extracts described in this book are whole food-produced without the use of noxious solvents and/or alcohol. However, this is not the case of commercial birch bark or chaga extracts, as demonstrated by the information in the next section.

Commercial extracts: the process

There are numerous commercial chaga extracts available. Many of these tout high levels of active ingredients. In fact, many boast massive ORAC levels. However, these extracts are usually heavily processed, and this accounts for their 'concentration.' In some cases the extracts are the result of cooking. This is in part to produce a powdery extract that makes an easy-to-use tea. Thus, rather than preservation of the active ingredients convenience is the objective. Consider the production of Chaga Honestea, a Japanese product. The chaga is cooked until it is well processed. Then, after cooling an enzyme, beta-1, 3 glucanase, is added. After this, the chaga is re-cooked. Finally, after drying it is packaged in tea-bags. The artificially added enzyme remains in the final product.

Another Japanese product, Chaga Super-High Grade capsules, is the result of a number of production steps. The same steps are taken, as mentioned previously. To make the final product polished rice is powdered, to which the yeast, *Monasus anka*, is added. This yeast, upon fermenting rice, gives the residue a reddish color. The rice/yeast mixture is fermented for two weeks. The final product is dried and ground into a powder. Then, this is mixed with the ground, cooked chaga and encapsulated. In Russia chaga undergoes similar processes. Thus, the only unprocessed, raw chaga and/or birch bark supplements available are the chaga/birch bark raw expresso and the raw emulsified chaga drops, the latter being available in a two-ounce dropper bottle.

Here is another method of production applied by Korean researchers. The mushroom is powdered. Then, the powder is boiled for *four hours*. After this, it is cooled to room temperature and then filtered. The extract is evaporated until completely dry, another heat-producing procedure. After this it is freeze-dried to create an easy-to-mix powder. This is the material used in Korean research. Obviously, four hours of intense heating destroys all enzymes and also destroys a certain amount of the vitamins. Furthermore, the sterols will be to a degree distorted by such an intensive heat-dependent extraction. This is why the raw extract emulsified in spice oils is preferable. In this form all the nutrients are intact, as is the molecular nature of the sterols and enzymes. Taken as sublingual drops this maximizes the absorption of the key active ingredients such as the sterols, phenolic compounds, enzymes, vitamins, and minerals.

There are even more severe methods of extraction than the use of prolonged heat. In some cases harsh solvents are used, largely because of their ability to emulsify or, rather, dissolve lipids. Then, the lipids are the primary active ingredients of both chaga and birch bark. In some cases the solvent of choice is alcohol, in others the petrochemical hexane. In still others methanol is the extracting agent, and this, of course, is the highly poisonous wood alcohol. While these may be largely driven off the final product through heat, still, residues remain. Regardless, no one can image that healthy product would result after soaking a natural medicine in harsh substances such as ethyl alcohol, methanol, and/or hexane.

Surely, for instance no one would do this consciously in their home. In other words, can anyone imagine, picking wild dandelion leaves, wild mushroom, or any other natural food, and then soaking them in gasoline, which is essentially the same as benzene? Then, why would anyone take an herb or natural food which is extracted in such a manner?

Chapter Four

Germs, Immunity, and More

While the folk use of this natural medicine is impressive, there is also significant modern proof. Scientific studies have demonstrated that chaga mushroom is exceedingly potent. In particular, these studies have demonstrated it has a high potency for strengthening the immune system. Yet, it also has germ-killing powers, and this is particularly true of the spice oil emulsion. The same is true of the spice oil emulsion of birch bark. Poplar bud extract is also a powerful germicide and is particularly active against viruses and fungi.

In particular, the chaga mushroom is largely an immune potentiator. In other words, it helps cause the immune system to be effective in its functions. All modern people suffer from impaired immunity. It might be said that it normalizes the immune response. Thus, all people would benefit from this action, because all modern people have lowered immunity, even before birth. Chaga mushroom, as the whole wild pulverized mushroom, fortified with wild white birch bark, as well as the emulsified whole mushroom drops, is precisely what people need to reverse this.

Regarding the immune system in every case where this mushroom was tested a positive result was seen. Then, these powerful results were without toxicity. The majority of the studies concern its effects against cancer cells. Here, too, it has been tested and found to be invaluable for cancer prevention, that is for the prevention of the toxin-induced mutations that lead to this disease. There are also studies which focus on immune strengthening actions. Additionally, chaga's capacity to fight inflammation has been evaluated. Here, too, positive results are seen. It has also been tested and found somewhat preventive against diabetes. Furthermore, a number of studies have evaluated its antioxidant powers, which are considerable. Analyzed nutritionally, it has been determined to be considerably dense, far more so than common or even organic foods.

It has also been evaluated for its germ-killing powers. Most studies have tested its capacity against viruses, where it scored well. However, it is also antiparasitic and antifungal. Of the forest cures the vast majority of the studies have been done on chaga mushroom and to a lesser degree birch bark. So, this will be the emphasis. Now, let us evaluate the details of these studies, so the true powers of this mushroom and its extracts can be comprehended.

Antiviral properties

Regarding forest cures both chaga mushroom and birch bark are antiseptics. In one study an extract of chaga demonstrated potent antiviral actions, particularly against influenza viruses. The substances responsible for this action were determined to be the phenolic compounds hispidin and hisolon. These phenolic substances are exclusive to chaga and birch bark. As well poplar bud extract is germicidal, particularly against the viruses of the herpes family.

While forest cures have a degree of germ-killing power this is not the main mechanism of action. Extracts of birch bark, that is of the bark itself, and the chaga mushroom, contain components that have a profound effect upon the human immune system. Chaga, as well as birch bark, are immune activators and are highly potent in this regard. So, they cause the immune system to function not merely normally but, actually, superiorly. Poplar bud extract also exerts this action. This is the key to vital health. Thus, now, finally, the immune system can perform at the optimal level to clear dangerous invaders, including sudden viruses but also those viruses which chronically infect the system. Studies have clearly shown that chaga activates the various immune cells to secrete powerful substances, such as interferon and interleukins, which then cause these cells to seek and destroy invaders. One way chaga and birch bark achieve this is by activating the powers of key antiviral and antitumor cells known as natural killer (NK) cells.

The emulsified chaga extract, as drops under the tongue, is the ideal antiviral medicine. This is superior to mere chaga itself. This is because it is emulsified with oil of wild oregano, and wild oregano oil itself is a potent antiviral agent. Studies by Microbiotest Labs have demonstrated that oil of wild oregano destroys in tissue culture cold viruses, flu viruses, and even the bird flu virus. Siddiqui and his group publishing in *Medical Science Research* demonstrated under the electron microscope the effects of oil of oregano against viruses. Here, he determined, the viruses were "disintegrated" by the oil, a result which was deemed "remarkable." He also found that clove and cinnamon oils caused disintegration. All such oils are found in the chaga spice oil emulsion. So, this combination, this direct killing plus the immune activation, is the ideal one for the ultimate destruction of viruses as well as the resolution of chronic viral diseases.

Yet, again, the major issue with chaga regarding viral diseases relates to its actions on the immune system. Obviously, for viruses to gain power over the body the immune system must be in dysfunction. Chaga and birch bark, both rich in biologically active sterols and in the case of chaga beta glucan, activate this system. Yet, these substances are so versatile in their actions that they also normalize immunity. Now, as a result of the intake of both these natural medicines the immune system can operate optimally. Through this therapy infestations of the body by viruses can be purged, a feat impossible to achieve by any other approach. Again, ideally the therapy with chaga and birch bark should be combined with wild oil of oregano and, possibly, the juice of wild oregano.

Regarding forest cures wild, raw multiple berries extracts, such as the maximum strength eight Canadian berries extract, are highly antiviral. So are individual wild berry extracts from certain antiseptic berries from the cranberry family. For instance, wild, raw lingonberry extract is a virus killer. Furthermore, wild sockeye salmon oil, polar-source, provides vitamin A, which is necessary for building the immune defense against these invaders. Whole unprocessed cod liver oil is another source of this vitamin. Even so, polar-source fatty salmon oil (as an eight-ounce bottle) is superior, because it is richer in vitamin A and D than cod liver oil, plus, as a rule, it is a far richer source of the full spectrum of omega-3s. Additionally, regarding such an oil this is a crude steam distilled extract, and, thus, it is far less refined than cod liver oil. Furthermore, it is the most stable of all fish oils, because of its rich content of astaxanthin. Look only for polar-source wild sockeye salmon oil that is rich in all categories of nutrients, that is the full spectrum of fatty acids, the omega-3s, the vitamin A, the vitamin D, and the astaxanthin.

Chronic viral infection leads to a wide range of diseases. For instance, fibromyalgia, multiple sclerosis, and chronic fatigue syndrome are largely due to such infestation. In such conditions the intake of chaga mushroom extract, birch bark extract, and wild, raw berries is a boon.

Antifungal powers

The antifungal powers of chaga extract are significant. This mushroom is a kind of plant-animal. Thus, it is a biological factory, which produces the ideal nutrients and phytochemicals for human use. It wants no competition, so it makes its own specialized compounds—in other words it creates antifungal agents, which are of immense value in human health.

These antifungal agents are highly potent. However, unlike antifungal drugs they are exceedingly safe. Thus, chaga extracts can be aggressively used to purge fungal infections from the body. This medicinal mushroom is so vigorous in its antifungal actions that it may be regarded as, essentially, an antifungal drug. Here, it is effective internally but also topically. For fungal disorders chaga can be used routinely. It is safe for all ages, and it is also safe to use for a prolonged period. Furthermore, it is safe for pregnant and nursing women, rather, it is exceedingly nourishing, since it is a true whole food.

Fungal infections are notoriously stubborn. Long-term use of drugs is dangerous, which demonstrates the value of natural extracts, which are non-toxic. Regardless, with chemical therapy the fungi develop a profound resistance against virtually all treatments. Chaga is unique, because of its mechanism of action. It contains substances which stimulate the sluggish immune system to purge the fungus. Furthermore, as mentioned previously it contains antifungal molecules, which are drug-like but unlike pharmaceuticals are entirely safe. Additionally, this novel complex contains a wide range of sterols, which are themselves antifungal agents. The sterols disrupt the cell membranes of the fungi, causing their death. Thus, there is no possibility of fungal resistance to this novel natural medicine. Rather, chaga, as well as birch bark, is an ideal treatment for drug resistant fungal infections.

To survive both chaga and birch bark must make antifungal chemicals. That plant sterols are antifungal should be no surprise, since the majority of today's fungus-killing drugs are of the same nature. Furthermore, they are derived from fungi. Antibiotics, too, are made from fungi. For instance, consider erythromycin. Made by Abbot Labs this drug is produced through growing fungi in enormous vats. The fungi produce this chemical, which is, then, extracted. Anyone driving by or living near the massive Abbot complex (North Chicago) where this drug is produced will know this. The area, depending on the direction of the wind, reeks of mold.

The need by fungi to produce antifungal agents and antibiotics is obvious. The purpose of these organisms is to cause decay, and all germs love such an environment. Fungi grow on rot. Without making these drugs there is no way these organisms could survive. In other words, they would be overwhelmed by competitors. Yet, incredibly, the same is true of humans. In order to thrive they, too, must be able to fend off any attackers.

With chaga it is somewhat different. This is a reparative fungus. Regarding the birch tree the whole purpose is to actually strengthen it rather than decay or destroy it. Even so, to protect itself from attack by other fungi it makes various antifungal agents.

This is demonstrated by modern research, in particular, work done on the antifungal substance rapamycin. This substance is a secretion of soil microbes, including certain types of fungi, found in the tropics. As reported in the *London Telegraph*, July 2009, this compound is a veritable longevity agent. American investigators found that rapamycin, when fed to aging mice, achieved a spectacular result. This was to increase life expectancy by nearly 30%. This was in male mice. Incredibly, in female mice it increase lifespan by 40%. Said A. Richardson, director, Barshop Institute of Longevity and Aging Studies, Texas, where much of this research was conducted, "I've been in aging research for 35 years, and there have been many so-called 'anti-aging' interventions over those years that were never successful. I never thought we would find an anti-aging pill for people in my lifetime. However, rapamycin shows a great deal of promise to do just that." Rapamycin acts through the same mechanism of action as chaga mushroom.

There was another key finding of the study. This is the fact that in the study the substance was given late in life, in comparative equivalents at some 60 human years. Yet, it still extended lifespan, as mentioned. Chaga has a similar mechanism of action as rapamycin, plus it contains the anti-aging enzyme SOD. This means that it is superior to rapamycin alone.

For such fungal extracts a mechanism of action is proposed. They contain substances which interfere with a gene-enzyme system that accelerates aging. This is a system known as TOR, which regulates the rate of metabolism in cells. This modulator of TOR greatly slows the aging process, because metabolism is the same as burning, that is the burning of oxygen, and this obviously increases the rate of decay. That is why a moderate cold climate is associated with a longer life. In other words, the cooling of the body slows oxygen burning. Even so, it is well known that an excessively high rate of metabolism is an aging factor. For instance, people with pathological forms of metabolic activity, such as those with adrenal tumors, cancer, leukemia, lymphoma, and/or hyperthyroidism, age virtually overnight.

Chaga is essentially a natural antifungal drug. In this regard it can compete with any fungus-killing pharmaceutical agent. Here, it is effective against chronic fungal infections. In particular, it is of immense value against psoriasis, eczema, dermatitis, vitiligo, alopecia, ringworm, vaginitis, prostatitis, and acne, all of which may be due to fungal infestation.

Anticancer properties

This is a disease which has largely been deemed incurable. There is no basis for this. When using natural medicines, such as chaga and birch bark, cancer cells, and even tumors, can be destroyed. Thus, the terminal nature of cancer is in dispute. There are countless millions of people whose cancers have been cured without noxious chemicals and/or procedures. This is through the use of natural methods, including diet, exercise, and herbal medicine. Extracts of wild spices, berries, greens, and mushrooms are potent antitumor agents and are also now being used in the treatment of cancerous diseases. Even the power of positive thinking has been found effective against this disease.

There are countless natural substances with cancer fighting properties. In fact, anything which enhances immunity is an aid against cancer. Mushrooms are particularly potent in this respect. Yet, there is a great difference between the mushrooms. For instance, chaga is far more powerful in the eradication of tumors than the more commonly known ones such as maitake and reishi. Even so, all such mushrooms are beneficial. It is just that chaga is the most aggressive and dependable. This is confirmed by herbalist David Winston who says that of all types of mushrooms chaga is the strongest in anti-cancer powers. In addition, according to Lindequest in his monograph the *Pharmacological Potential of Mushrooms* in eastern Europe birch tree fungi have played "an important role in prevention and treatment of cancer." This is of critical importance. Prevention is the real goal. Chaga is ideal in this regard. To achieve this it should be consumed daily or at least every other day, as both the sublingual emulsified drops and the expresso.

In eastern Europe and Russia the historical use of chaga for cancer is considerable. Since the 1500s the local people have relied on it to cure various cancers. This coincides with the science, since, without doubt the mushroom exhibits antitumor properties. Rather, it is even more profound than this, because components of chaga actually destroy cancer cells. Says Lindequest, "Antitumor effects of several extracts and isolated compounds could be demonstrated in tumor cell systems and in animal assays." Then, he notes, this power is to be expected, since chaga has a number of natural steroids, which block tumor growth—and as he reveals it also has an enzyme, ergosterol peroxide, which is a cancer fighter. Additionally, of all mushrooms or natural substances chaga alone has the melanin complex, which has "high antioxidant" activity and which, thus, protects the genes—the DNA—from toxin-induced degeneration.

Regardless, there is no doubt about it chaga is one of those rare whole food complexes which is capable of regenerating the immune system. Its key components, notably the sterols, polysaccharides, phenolic compounds, and polysaccharide-amino acid complexes, are capable of activating the immune response. This activation is against a wide range of invaders, including viruses, fungi, yeasts, and bacteria as well as cancer cells.

Regarding activation against cancer cells the polysaccharides and polysaccharide-amino acid complexes, for instance, the beta glucans, are particularly powerful. These compounds, found in rich supplies in chaga, activate action-oriented cells, including macrophages, T lymphocytes, and NK killer cells, to perform their role superiorly. In this regard it has been demonstrated that the mushroom components increase the secretion by these cells of key immune modulating compounds, including cytokines. The cytokines are special molecules secreted by white blood cells. This is in response to stress, particularly that caused by infection and/or cancer. Some of these cytokines induced by chaga mushroom include tumor necrosis factor, interleukin, and interferon. All these chemicals activate the immune cells to purge the body of invaders. Yet, these chemical mediators also serve a most invaluable function. This is because the cytokines combat the excessive growth of cells. This is why chaga and its extracts are so invaluable for the destruction of cancerous growths and also for the reversal of eczema and psoriasis.

Note also the mediator tumor necrosis factor. This speaks for itself. The body seeks to consume cancer. It merely needs a boost. By accelerating the production of tumor necrosis factor, necrosis meaning "to kill or cause to decay," obviously, nothing could be more powerful in the battle against cancer than this. It would appear that the entire purpose of chaga is to assist the body in the eradication of tumors. This coincides with early Polish research, which determined that the mushroom has the capacity to directly and preferentially kill tumor cells by, incredibly, causing the consumption of their nuclei.

Truly, it is in the nature of chaga to be a tumor fighter. It grows on the bark of white and black birch trees, which are true survivors. These trees thrive in harsh climates such as the northern forests of Russia and Canada. The mushroom itself thrives in such climates and fails to grow in the more southerly region of birch growth. In modern society this is a challenge. Since it is such a powerful survivor and since it can overwhelm even these hardy trees, chaga has one of the most powerful immune systems of all creation. Thus, by consuming it people can benefit from its immune compounds. They can also benefit by increasing their immune surveillance against dangerous cancer cells.

Does anyone know how a person can remain in good health and can, therefore, ward off disease? Too, how can a person guard themselves from the major killers, particularly cancer? One such way is to keep the immune system at a heightened level of activity. It is good to have an active immune system. In contrast, it is a sluggish immunity which is the root of all sickness.

Doctors spread misinformation about this. They say that too active of an immune system is dangerous. This leads, they proclaim, to autoimmune disease. This explains the attempt by physicians to suppress the immune system with potent drugs. Yet, this approach is catastrophic. It is the sluggish or incompetent immune system which is the cause of disease. In contrast, a highly powerful one, an active one, is precisely the source of prevention.

In this regard chaga is invaluable. This mushroom creates its own powerful immunity for survival. After all, it thrives on birch trees, which are among the most hardy plants in the world. Chaga produces enzymes, which halt inflammation. This is invaluable for healthy immunity. When consumed by humans, it induces the production of interferons, which then serve to activate a healthier immune response. As well, interferons stimulate the repair of DNA, and this repair is necessary so the chromosomes can remain healthy.

There is another reason this mushroom is invaluable to the immune system, in fact, the entire body. This relates to oxygen metabolism. Chaga's active ingredients are highly oxygenated. This includes the cholesterol molecules known as sterols. Chaga thrives in an oxygen-rich environment, and it makes chemicals which trap this precious nutrient.

Perhaps the work of Polish investigators gives the most ideal summary of chaga's anticancer powers. Rzymowska of the Polish Medical Academy did a study on the effect of this mushroom on the genetics of cancer. This researcher found that the extract "inhibited the growth of tumor cells," in this case cervical cancer cells. Noted Rzymowska chaga extract "disturbed the metabolism in (cancer) cells" by blocking enzymes necessary for cancer cell growth, while simultaneously increasing the amount of enzyme in the cells, notably catalase, which aid in cancer cell destruction. Ultimately, chaga caused a reduction in cancer cell growth, leading to the breakdown in the tumor.

How to treat cancer with natural medicine

Chemotherapy and radiation therapy are poor choices for the treatment of this disease. The disease is caused by toxicity as well as germs. How can the use of substances or methods which destroy the immune system and also intoxicate the body aid in the cure? This is a hoax. The mere presumption that they will cure is, perhaps, more responsible for any benefit rather than any direct effect of such approaches. The exception may be naturally-derived chemotherapy agents, such as Taxol and the various alkaloids, because these drugs are to a degree germicidal.

The role of germs in the cause of cancer is well established. Suffice it to say that a wide range of germs, upon infesting the body, cause this disease. There are usually other factors, such as stress and chemical toxicity, which participate in the cause. Yet, the microbes are a major cause of the biochemical and inflammatory reactions which lead to the development of tumors.

Surely, in the development of cancer another key factor is poor diet. In particular, the intake of refined sugar and vegetable oils is a cancer factor of a vast degree, as is the consumption of nitrated meats. Additionally, pork flesh readily induces this disease. Furthermore, noxious pollutants, such as benzene derivatives, toluene, PCBs, dioxins, vinyl chloride, pesticides, herbicides, fungicides, synthetic dyes, and asbestos, are known carcinogens. In addition, exposure to X-rays, nuclear irradiation, depleted uranium, and natural radium are significant risk factors. In fact, the combination of poor diet plus consistent exposure to such toxins/irradiation often leads to the disease.

Treatment protocol

To treat this condition take the wild, raw emulsified chaga drops, 50 to 100 drops three times daily. Also, take the chaga/birch bark expresso, one cup twice daily. Furthermore, take the wild, raw birch bark emulsion, 50 to 100 drops twice daily. Consume also the emulsified poplar bud extract, 50 to 100 drops twice daily, In addition, wild, raw forest berries are potent antitumor agents, especially when converted into extracts. These extracts are taken as drops under the tongue. Take wild, raw eight berry extract made from remote-source Canadian wild berries, 100 drops under the tongue three times daily. Also, consume the wild, raw black raspberry extract (rubus species), as drops in a two-ounce bottle, 50 to 100 drops twice daily. In addition, consume the wild juice of oregano and juice of rosemary, one ounce of each twice daily. The latter is a rare supplement available only in limited quantities. In cancers of the colon, mouth, female organs, and kidneys wild, raw lingonberry drops may be added, 50 drops twice daily. For the infectious component take the oil of wild oregano in extra virgin olive oil, ten drops three or more times daily under the tongue. This is a powerful protocol for the eradication of cancerous growths as well as for the boosting of the immune system against such disease.

Never give up hope. For all cancers natural cures must be used, particularly the chaga extracts and wild, raw berry drops, to destroy this disease. The infection(s) must also be purged, and for this purpose the wild oregano extracts must be consumed, largely in the form of oil of wild oregano (Mediterranean wild hand-picked) and the juice of oregano. Note: more will be discussed later in the section on cancer.

Chapter Five

Diseases and their Forest Cures

There are thousands of diseases which are resistant to modern medicines. This demonstrates the crucial nature of natural medicines, which offer vast hope for such conditions. A few of the key diseases are listed in this chapter, especially those known to respond to prominent forest cures such as bark and bud extracts as well as chaga. The cures are based both upon scientific studies and actual human use, including the ethnic use by societies which largely discovered these cures.

Psoriasis—a kind of skin cancer?

This is a complex disease. It is also stubborn. Generally, it is difficult to cure. People make every attempt to eliminate it, but usually their efforts fail. Largely, they lose hope, which is understandable. Yet, chaga gives much hope. This is because it activates the immune system so that the psoriatic lesions can be cleared.

In part psoriasis is due to infection of the skin tissues. Germs which act as perpetrators include *Pitysporum ovale*, Staph epidermidis, Staph aureus, streptococcus, and *Candida albicans*. Rosenburg at the University of Tennessee Knoxville scraped and cultured all such germs from psoriatic plaques. However, the ultimate cause is a collapse of the immune system from chronic infection, toxicity, and stress.

The psoriasis plaques are like a kind of skin tumor. They are represented by excessive, toxic growth of skin cells. This is an overgrowth of cells due to a stimulus, and one of these stimuli is cancer. In other words, psoriasis may be an obvious sign of a hidden tumor. Another hidden factor is fungal and/or bacterial infection of the skin as well as such infestation in the lower small intestines. Yet another is infestation of the gut, liver, and/or lungs by parasites.

Thus, systemic infection, particularly infection of the liver and/or gut but also infestation of the glands, is highly common in this disease. Here, fungal forms are the primary culprits, although noxious bacteria and parasites may also play a role. Surprisingly, there may be an underlying infection by TB as the cause of this disease. There may be infection by TB in the intestine and/or bones. Furthermore, a candida yeast infection of the bowel or blood may also be the primary progenitor. Additionally, for psoriasis to develop there is usually severe stress, so the coping mechanisms of the body have failed. This means that in many cases it is preceded by collapse of the endocrine system. Once the glands become weakened it is then that they become infected. This is by fungi, pleomorphic bacteria, and/or tubercular pathogens. There is also the issue of toxicity, particularly toxic overload of the liver and colon.

Vaccines are also a major cause of psoriasis. These injections destabilize immunity, causing a vast degree of corruption in the body. This leads to a weakening of the body's resistance to stress, and, thus, in people who have received numerous vaccines a major stressor can lead to dire consequences. These consequences of vaccines plus stress include the development of diabetes, inflammation of the lungs, chronic bronchitis, multiple sclerosis, psoriasis, eczema, alopecia, immune suppression, Crohn's disease, spastic colon, ulcerative colitis, pericarditis, arteritis, ankylosing spondylitis, and arthritis. Regardless, the majority of people who develop severe psoriasis and/or eczema have been vaccinated.

Even so, for infection to develop in the skin there must be underlying disease. The infection of psoriasis is a sign of immune breakdown. It is a sign that the entire immune system is disabled by, for instance, stress, toxicity, and/or infestation. Thus, the regeneration of the immune system is the real cure for the reversal of this disease. This is why emulsified extracts of chaga mushroom and birch bark are essential for the cure. The stress, too, must be reversed. People with the disease must learn to relax completely in order to assist in the cure.

That psoriasis lesions may represent what is known as an occult, that is a hidden, tumor is well published. As mentioned previously these lesions may also be a sign of parasitic infestation of the bowel wall as well as liver. If the cancerous tissue and/or parasitic infestation is purged, the psoriasis disappears. This purging may certainly require the intake of the birch bark and chaga but also necessitates the intake of a purging agent made from wild, raw greens, remote-source spice oils, and heavy monounsaturated oils such as extra virgin olive oil and black seed oil. Also, wild juice of oregano is a potent supplement for purging such invaders. Vitamin A and D deficiency is yet another factor to consider. These vitamins help regulate the growth of skin cells as well as the cells of the mucous membranes. The connection with vitamin D is made obvious by the effects of sunlight on this disorder, since psoriasis usually improves in the summer. Vitamin D can be gained also through supplements, notably the intake of polar-source fatty salmon oil (steam extracted).

With its immune activating powers chaga provides much hope for this disease. According to U. Lindequist and his group at the Institute of Pharmacy, Greifwald, Germany, whole food extracts of this mushroom have demonstrated actions against skin pathogens, including the ubiquitous Pitysporum. Russian investigators have determined that it is active also against TB. Additionally, the chaga polysaccharides, for instance, beta glucan, induce the production of chemical mediators which specifically activate the immune cells against psoriatic plaques. Furthermore, extracts of chaga have been demonstrated to destroy bizarre cell growth, as occurs in psoriasis. Thus, chaga mushroom is a kind of purge for this disease.

Again, the psoriasis cure is based upon more than merely killing any germs. This is because in psoriasis there is a vast dilemma. This is the fact that the immune system on its own cannot clear the disease. Thus, essentially the immune system is in a failure mode. Rather, it has been neutralized. Enter the value of forest cures, especially chaga mushroom, birch bark emulsion, and the emulsified poplar bud extract. These forest medicines greatly boost the natural powers of the immune system. Now, the white blood cells and various lymph cells can operate efficiently. They, with their new-found power, can go about cleansing the body of all toxins, including mutated/psoriatic cells. This is a sophisticated way to eradicate this oppressive disease. The person can simply keep boosting the immunity. This is so that on its own the body will clear this disease. Once and for all as a result of the systematic use of chaga extracts this disease can be obliterated.

Detoxification also assists in the cure of psoriasis. In particular, as mentioned previously purging of toxins from the liver is crucial. So is the dissolution and/or purging of gallstones. People with psoriasis commonly have such stones. They also usually suffer from deep-seated parasitic infestation. In addition, usually psoriatics suffer from sluggish kidney function. A purging agent is available which naturally cleanses these organs without any harshness. This is a purge made from wild raw forest greens in a base of organic extra virgin olive oil, black seed oil, raw, wild high bush cranberry, and organic raw apple cider vinegar. The regular intake of such a formulation will usually cause the dumping of noxious parasites into the stool. Also, this purges from the body poisonous chemicals and heavy metals, which disrupt cellular metabolism and, thus, impair healing. Thus, the intake of an ounce of this purge in the morning before breakfast for 30 or more days assists in the psoriasis cure.

Emulsions of chaga and birch bark are essential. These are taken as sublingual drops. The chaga in particular may be rubbed on the lesions and is particularly soothing, largely due to the rich content of sterols. Regarding psoriasis the powers of this mushroom are truly remarkable. In fact, nothing in nature is as powerful as emulsified chaga extract in the relief and reversal of this disease.

It is critical to reiterate. Emulsified chaga extract is essentially a cure for this condition. This is particularly true when it is combined with the total body purging agent. The extract may be taken as drops under the tongue or simply be swallowed. The wild chaga/birch bark expresso or tea should also be consumed. Also, it may be necessary to consume white birch bark, as drops under the tongue. Furthermore, the chaga emulsion can be applied topically and is highly soothing. Both chaga and wild birch bark are potent antifungal agents.

Treatment protocol

To eradicate this disease patience is required. Even so, the combination therapy, as follows, is a relatively quick cure, listed in priority:

- wild, raw chaga spice oil emulsion: 40 or more drops under the tongue twice daily; also, rub this emulsion into psoriatic lesions
- total body purging agent, consisting of wild raw forest greens emulsified in heavy monounsaturated oils plus raw apple cider vinegar: an ounce or more daily
- wild, raw chaga expresso: one cup twice daily
- wild, raw white birch bark emulsion: 80 drops twice daily
- oil of wild oregano: five drops under the tongue twice daily
- emulsion of wild, raw poplar buds in extra virgin olive oil and raw apple cider vinegar: 40 drops under the tongue or by mouth twice daily
- healthy bacterial supplement (Ecologic 500 strain): as directed

Herpes

Traditionally, in eastern Europe and Russia chaga is used for this infection. This makes sense, since this mushroom boosts the immune system's capacity to eradicate viruses.

Herpes is a modern plague. The virus readily infects the nervous system, where it hides. Under stress it becomes activated and tears through the nerves, causing inflammation and pain. The blister(s) seen on the surface is only the final component of the infection. Much of the herpes epidemic is the result of vaccinations, which have introduced the germ as a contaminant. Furthermore, these shots cause immune suppression, which allows the virus to thrive.

The key with herpes is to eradicate the infection. This is from the deepest recesses of the body. This requires the massive activation of the immune system because, again, this virus hides in the nerves, specifically the nerve bodies known as ganglia. In addition, spice oils must be consumed which are antiviral. The most potent of these are oil of wild oregano and oil of wild bay leaf. In addition to being antiviral these oils are highly antiinflammatory. They are also analgesic, meaning they ease pain. Plus, the oil of wild oregano when taken as sublingual drops helps purge the herpes virus from its repository, which is the deep-seated nerve ganglia of the body. Also, poplar bud contains potent analgesics as well as antiinflammatory agents. Furthermore, the resin of poplar contains highly potent antiviral agents, including caffeic acid and benzoic acid. Thus, this is one of the most powerful natural medicines for destroying the herpes virus, while also eliminating the agonizing symptoms, particularly when consumed as an emulsion (in extra virgin olive oil and raw apple cider vinegar).

Shingles is a herpes virus infection. While this condition causes devastating pain and inflammation it is no match to the powers of wild forest cures. The poplar bud extract, as well as the emulsions of chaga and birch bark, are all highly effective against this disease. So is oil of wild oregano (super-strength concentration), which actually destroys the herpes/shingles virus. Additionally, a wild, raw source of vitamins A and D is essential. This aids in the regeneration of the mucous membranes as well as the production of antibodies, which are essential mechanisms to protect against this infection. Take wild fresh water cod (burbot) liver oil, about a half teaspoon twice daily or as drops 20 drops under the tongue twice daily.

Treatment protocol

Take emulsified wild chaga drops, 20 drops under the tongue several times daily. Also, drink the chaga/birch bark expresso, one cup twice daily. Additionally, take oil of wild oregano, five drops under the tongue several times daily. Rub the emulsified chaga drops and/or oil of oregano over any infected site. For cold sores saturate cotton with the emulsified drops and hold over the lesion. For genital herpes the oregano is excessively hot, but the chaga emulsion may be tolerated; dilute four parts to one with water, and apply to lesions often. Furthermore, take oil of wild oregano in a super/high strength form, five drops under the tongue a few times daily. Rub or dab the oil on any lesions.

Consume also oil of wild bay leaf in an extra virgin olive oil base, twenty drops under the tongue three or more times daily. Also use this oil topically, as needed. For shingles take the wild, raw chaga emulsion, 40 drops under the tongue several times daily. Also, rub this on any painful regions. Take also the emulsified poplar bud extract, 40 drops repeatedly. In addition, take the super/high-strength oil of wild oregano, 20 drops under the tongue repeatedly, and also apply this to any painful region. For shingles the adrenal glands must be supported; take undiluted royal jelly capsules fortified with pantothenic acid, four capsules several times daily. Be sure to also use plenty of sea salt, as this boosts adrenal function. The consumption of refined sugar should be banned, as this toxin devastates adrenal function and increases the likelihood for herpes virus invasion.

Tuberculosis

This is one of the most difficult of all diseases to cure. It is also one of the most difficult to diagnose. People can easily contract it from hospitalized patients or through airline travel. It can also be contracted through vaccines, particularly the live TB vaccine known as BCG. This vaccine, banned in the United States, is commonly given in Canada as well as England.

It is important to reiterate that this disease is far more common than is realized—and it is reasonable to estimate that a many as one of three people globally have at least some element of this disease. Thus, when there are symptoms of TB even at a low level, it is a good idea to treat it. This is through the intake of potent wild spice extracts, such as oil of wild oregano, the multiple spice extract, and the juice of wild oregano, along with chaga. Low level symptoms and signs of TB include stiffness of the neck, swelling of the upper thoracic region, scoliosis, feeling of being hot, especially in the afternoon, fatigue, muscle weakness, clubbing of the nail beds, and night sweats.

Chaga is a potent cure for this condition, as is the wild-source birch bark. In Russia and Siberia this mushroom has even been used successfully for TB of the bone, which is notoriously difficult to treat. In Poland chaga is a front-line therapy for tuberculosis. When combined with white birch bark, it is a highly effective anti-tubercular medicine.

The effectiveness of this mushroom against this disease is profound. The reason for its power relates to the immune system, which it so dramatically activates. The TB bacillus neutralizes the immune system to such a degree that this system can no longer clear it. All this is changed through the intake of chaga, because, now, finally, the immune system is activated sufficiently to clear the pathogen.

There is a warning regarding this. Many people with TB are weak. The chaga and wild white birch bark tea is exceedingly potent. Along with the sublingual drops of wild oregano and the juice of oregano this will target the precise areas of sickness. Thus, there may be a slight increase in symptoms or, perhaps, new symptoms. Regardless, these changes are never serious and must be merely tolerated until the cure is achieved. Furthermore, if any unusual symptoms develop, the person should never stop the therapy. In contrast, this therapy should be accelerated and the amount of chaga extract should be doubled or tripled. Symptoms of such detoxification reactions include rash, fever, night sweats, and flu-like symptoms.

For tuberculosis chaga therapy works best with wild oregano treatment. While chaga activates the immune system against the pathogens which cause this disease oregano extracts offer a direct killing action. A study done at Georgetown University proves that in petri dishes wild oil of oregano, Mediterranean-source, kills tubercular germs. Like chaga, this spice has a prolonged history for use in TB. In the 1500s in medieval England a variety of herbalists reported that a special kind of wild oregano extract, the oregano juice, was a cancer cure. Additionally, the emulsified wild chaga drops contain wild oil of oregano.

Regardless, both chaga and birch bark extracts offer massive powers against this disease. There is little available which curbs it, rather, reverses it. This is true even with natural medicines. Against tuberculosis tree medicines have a direct and measurable effect. They give the body great power to fight this resistant infection. Actually, chaga alone has been used successfully to reverse TB of the bone, a fact which is highly significant. Of all mushrooms only chaga has the capacity to vigorously purge this pathogen, even from the deepest recesses of the body, that is even from within the bone. In the cure it should ideally be combined with emulsified extract of wild birch bark, along with oil of wild oregano and the oregano juice. Crude whole food vitamin D is also invaluable, ideally in the form of wild sockeye salmon oil or burbot liver oil—or both. The salmon oil should be steam-distilled and unfiltered. It should be polar in source and rich in vitamins A and D as well as astaxanthin. The burbot oil is cold-fermented from remote regions of the far north; the burbot holds no contaminants and is also an excellent source of vitamin K. Vitamins A, D, and K are essential to build strong bone as well as a strong immune system. For tough cases both these oils should be consumed. Finally, as a result of the aforementioned protocol effective medicines are available to eradicate this plague of humanity and, therefore, save countless lives.

The action of chaga against TB relates to its nutritional density as well as its actions on the immune system. Nutritionally, it offers dense amount of highly biologically active sterols, which exert a direct effect against the tubercular germ. When absorbed into the cell walls of the TB organisms, these sterols weaken the germs, making them easier to kill. The sterols have the opposite effect on healthy cells, because they strengthen them and, thus, make them more resistant to invasion by TB. Also, with chaga the rich content of SOD is critical, since this oxygen-rich enzyme assists the body in purging the smoldering TB pathogens. That is why people were eventually cured when placed in sanitoriums away from the cities in fresh air. The use of fresh raw milk is also related to oxygen, since this food is rich in the oxygen-metabolizing vitamin riboflavin. Thus, the ingestion of foods/supplements rich in biologically active forms of oxygen—molecular oxygen—is a major component of the cure of this disease.

Mushrooms, especially those which grow on trees, have a prolonged use in the treatment of this dreaded disease. Some 2000 years ago the Greek physician Dioscorides included the larch tree fungus, *Fomitopsis officinalis*, in his dispensary. He held it as a specific cure for tuberculosis, including TB of the bone and lungs. Chaga mushroom has an even more predominant usage for this purpose. It was the ancient Chinese, about 4500 B.C., who found it effective against tuberculosis of the bones. Prior to this it was the infamous Ice Man, found frozen amidst the melting glaciers of the Alps, who demonstrated his preference in natural pharmacy. In his possession was a chaga-like mushroom, known as the birch polyspore fungus, *Piptoporus betulinus*. This is similar to chaga. Yet, of all tree fungi chaga is the most potent. Moreover, despite the Russian use recent studies demonstrate that Canadian-source chaga is even more potent than the Siberian type. This is the type used in the wild, raw emulsified chaga drops as well as the wild chaga/birch bark expresso. This tremendously powerful natural medicine is capable of rooting the TB germ from the body. To reiterate as demonstrated by its historical use in Europe and Russia it is even capable of doing so from the bone, which is a key repository for tuberculosis. The TB germ hides there and when the opportunity is ripe, it then is seeded to the rest of the body, including the lungs. Thus, the only way to cure TB is to destroy it in its repository. Chaga is effective, because it activates the rather sluggish immune response against this pathogen. In this respect this mushroom, as a fatty emulsion and also as a tea, is an essential treatment for this disease. For tough cases it is also essential to consume the oil of wild oregano (Mediterranean-source, wild hand-picked), the juice of oregano, and birch bark emulsion.

Treatment protocol

With orthodox medicine this is a tough disease to treat. The drugs are often more toxic than the disease, and it usually takes a prolonged period to eradicate it. Patience and persistence is required. Instead of drugs take emulsion of wild, raw chaga, 40 drops under the tongue four times daily. Also, take the wild, raw birch bark emulsion, 40 drops under the tongue four times daily (may ideally be taken at the same time). Consume oil of wild oregano (super-strength), 40 drops twice daily. Also, consume the wild oregano juice, one or more ounces daily.

The wild chaga expresso should also be consumed, about a cup twice daily. For vitamins A and D the ideal source is wild remote-source sockeye salmon oil, a tablespoonful or more daily. Additionally, the fresh water cod, that is burbot, liver oil must be consumed, a teaspoonful or more daily. Also, the wild raw triple greens flushing agent, rich in oxygenating riboflavin, must be taken, about 40 drops twice daily. For tough cases the dessicated multiple spice capsules must be added, about three capsules three times daily. This protocol is sufficient to eradicate TB in the majority of the cases. However, for TB of the bone also the spine should be rubbed with super-strength oil of oregano once or twice daily. Plus, the intake of the juice of oregano should be increased to up to four ounces daily. The intake of chaga mushroom expresso also should be increased to three cups daily. In some cases it is necessary to give mega-doses of wild salmon oil: two or three tablespoons daily.

Historically, dark green leafy greens have been used as a part of the cure. This may largely be due to the fact that they are highly nourishing as well as readily digested. It may be specifically related to the riboflavin content of such greens as a key vitamin. This vitamin is essential for the creation of cellular energy as well as for the efficient metabolism of oxygen. Without riboflavin the cells become greatly stressed and begin to degenerate. This is because, without the vitamin, there is no way for the cells to internally create energy.

While organic greens are a good source of this vitamin a far more rich source is wild greens. Plus, the wild greens in a raw state have a potent cleansing power, particularly on the gall bladder and liver, which tend to be sluggish in tuberculosis patients. Thus, a wild, raw triple greens flushing agent should be consumed, about 40 to 60 drops twice daily, as sublingual drops. For tough cases the amount can be increased to 100 drops three times daily.

This triple greens contains extract of wild burdock leaves. Burdock is a strong plant, and much of its strength is in its leaves. One of its powers is to cleanse the blood and also induce sweating. Both these functions are necessary for the cure of TB. Another wild greens cure is juice of wild, raw nettle (12-ounce bottle). The nettles are rich in riboflavin and also protein. Thus, this is a highly nourishing natural medicine for the weak and debilitated, including those suffering from tuberculosis.

Again, it should be kept in mind that this is not an easy disease to treat. Nor is it easy to quickly cure. The ultimate cure takes a prolonged time. One key to this is consistency. People with TB consistently need a good diet plus fresh air. Too, they also routinely need sunshine. Furthermore, any natural medicines which are effective must be taken as a routine. Failure to take even a daily dose has untoward effects.

The diet should be rich in fatty foods and low in grains. It should also be rich in high protein foods such as organically-raised meat and also wild fish. Organic whole milk and whole milk yogurt should be consumed on a regular basis. All foods selected should be rich in nutrients. Refined sugar and alcoholic beverages should be eliminated. In particular, chocolate should be avoided, as this is an endocrine stimulant which ultimately weakens the body. In addition, all sources of caffeine, that is coffee, black tea, and green tea, should be avoided. Instead, antiseptic teas, such as wild oregano (Mega-Orega) and sage teas (Sage-o-Soothe), should be consumed, since they are soothing rather than stimulating and are also strengthening and nourishing. Regarding wild oregano and sage these help strengthen bone and also activate the immune system. Thus, their regular consumption as a pulverized tea, a kind of tea infusion, will greatly increase the strength and resistance of the body. The natural medicines which must be taken on a daily basis include wild sockeye salmon oil, steam-distilled (rich in vitamins A and D), the juice of wild oregano, the oil of wild oregano, birch bark emulsion, and wild, raw chaga drops as well as the chaga/birch bark expresso. All these natural medicines must be taken on a daily basis, that is until a thorough cure is achieved.

What is the maintenance dose? The ideal is to continue to take these natural medicines daily or a few times weekly but merely in a lesser dose. At least one-half or one-third the original amount is needed. It varies per case, but, again, TB is tough and slow-growing.

Not everyone has access to fresh air and sunshine routinely. Here, there is the issue of city living, which ultimately compromises the function of the lungs as well as immunity. Nor is wholesome food available for most people continuously. Thus, the natural medicines described in this section fill this void. For those who are unable to manage their environment to the ideal the aforementioned natural medicines should be taken perhaps permanently. Regardless, chaga emulsion is the source of vast hope for the people who suffer from chronic disease. This is because it is one of the few natural complexes which vigorously regenerates the immune system.

Arthritis

Chaga, especially when taken in a spice oil-based fatty emulsion, is a potent treatment for this condition. Poplar bud extract is another highly powerful cure. The two together are a powerful team in the reversal of this disease.

Tree medicines contain a wide range of substances which are highly antiinflammatory. These substances are used by the trees to keep them healthy against the stresses of life. The biological compounds in trees are significantly more powerful than those typically found in smaller plants such as shrubs and herbs. For instance, the most popular of all pain medicines, aspirin, is a synthetic version of salicin, which was originally discovered in white willow bark. In fact, white willow bark was used by the Native Americans for pain, and this is how modern humans learned of it. Poplar bud extract is rich in this pain-killing substance. Other antiinflammatory substances found in tree medicines include proanthocyanidins, simple phenols, flavonoids, organic acids, tannins, sterols, and enzymes.

No doubt, arthritis is inflammatory. Yet, the question is what causes the inflammation? This is largely infection. Then, the infection is the result of the weakened or incompetent immune system. Thus, arthritis is ultimately caused by immune failure.

Chaga and birch bark restore this immunity. This is largely through their rich content of biologically potent sterols, which help activate sluggish immunity. Note: this activation is of value in all diseases, including so-called autoimmune disorders. Yet, regarding the reversal of arthritis in particular the content of SOD in chaga is of critical importance, since it is well established that this oxygen-bearing enzyme helps eliminate the inflammation associated with this disease. Simultaneously, this essential enzyme helps normalize the immune response, which is often aberrant in inflammatory connective tissue diseases. It does so by strengthening the capacity of this system to purge noxious pathogens, cleanse toxic substances, and reduce or eliminate inflammation. To achieve this the chaga must be taken regularly for a significant period of time, for instance, 90 days.

The sterols in chaga and birch bark are additional components for combating arthritis. Sterols are waxes and, thus, they serve a kind of lubricating function. They also stabilize cell walls. This means they prevent the production of chemicals, which cause inflammation. It also means that these sterols help prevent degenerative changes in the joints.

For arthritis another key natural medicine is extract of poplar bud. The poplar tree synthesizes powerful pain-killing substances, notably salicin (aspirin) and caffeic acid as well as benzoic acid. The bud of poplar is a concentrate of such substances. What's more, poplar bud is a powerful antioxidant with strong antiinflammatory powers. This is largely due to its rich content of phenolic compounds such as caffeic and cinnaminic acids. Thus, such phenolic power is invaluable for halting the toxicity and inflammation associated with this disease.

Treatment protocol

Take emulsified wild chaga drops, 40 drops twice daily. Take also emulsified birch bark extract, 40 drops twice daily. Additionally, take oil of oregano, five drops twice daily. Furthermore, drink the chaga/birch bark expresso, one cup daily. Also, consume the raw emulsified extract of poplar bud in a base of raw apple cider vinegar and extra virgin olive oil, 40 or more drops twice daily. For topical treatment the super-strength oregano oil can be used.

Rub the oil vigorously on the joints as often as possible. Vitamin C and flavonoids are needed to maintain joint health. The best source of vitamin C is a combination of wild camu camu and acerola cherry. Take a wild camu camu- and acerola-based vitamin C; consume about 200 to 300 mg daily.

AIDS

This is a disease due to a multiplicity of infections. Thus, substances which greatly activate the immune system are essential. So are germicides with broad-spectrum actions such as poplar bud extract and oil of wild oregano.

Regarding chaga there have been a number of studies, which have demonstrated an efficacy against the AIDS virus. As reported by investigators at Duke University

Medical Center a chaga derivative (a synthetic form of betulinic acid) is "a potent HIV-1 entry inhibitor."

There is strong proof for chaga's power against this infection. A number of studies have shown that this medicinal mushroom directly purges this virus from tissues.

A water extract of chaga has been shown to be effective against this disease. This is known as chaga/birch bark tea or expresso. Again, it is a quickly made infusion of chaga and birch bark in just boiled water. Even so, the infusion can also be made with steam. Another form which is active against this disease is the raw chaga mushroom emulsion.

It is well established that certain mushrooms possess substances with anti-HIV activities, for instance, as reported for *Lentinus edodes* by a number of researchers such as T. Tochikura in *Medical Microbiology and Immunology*. Yet, in this regard certain medicinal mushrooms are more powerful than others. Chaga is one of these. In 1998 T. Ichimura and his group, publishing in *Bioscience, Biotechnology, and Biochemistry* found that water soluble compounds in this mushroom, notably lignans, are highly active against HIV. Specifically, these lignans block the substance, HIV-protease, used by this virus to invade immune cells. Through this chaga extracts protect the lymphocytes from the virus' destructive effects.

Yet, there is also a great power of chaga in activating the immune response against this virus. Plus, it activates immunity against fungal infections, which are coincident with HIV. Furthermore, extracts of this mushroom, particularly a hot water expresso and the spice oil emulsion, assist in the regeneration of cell membranes. This is by supplying much needed sterols for structural support. In AIDS the cell membranes are entirely disrupted. Only chaga and birch bark extracts have the power to rebuild them. Moreover, the sterols of chaga and birch bark aid in the conduction of electrical impulses in the cell walls, which also aid in cellular regeneration.

There is no doubt about it medicinal mushrooms inhibit the synthesis of the HIV virus in human cells. The sterols and polysaccharides in these mushrooms are largely responsible for this action. These mushrooms, particularly chaga, also block the ability of the AIDS virus to enter or invade cells.

Treatment protocol

Take the wild, raw chaga mushroom emulsion, 50 to 100 drops three times daily. Take also the chaga/birch bark expresso, two or more cups daily. Additionally, take the wild, raw birch bark emulsion, 50 to 100 drops twice daily. The wild oregano oil must be consumed, about 20 drops three times daily under the tongue. The multiple spice extract made from dessicated oils of oregano, sage, cumin, and cinnamon is a highly potent natural medicine against this virus and its associated infections: take two or three capsules of this dessicated spice oil complex three times daily. Also, take poplar bud emulsion, about 40 drops twice daily.

Chronic otitis media (inner ear infection)

In this condition there is both infection and inflammation. Chronic allergy also plays a role. The sinus cavities are usually disrupted and/or inflamed, leading to dysfunction of the Eustachian tube and, thus, chronic inner ear infection.

Chaga mushroom emulsion is an ideal natural medicine for this condition. This is because it boosts the local immune response against this infection/inflammation, essentially purging it. The benefit of such an emulsion is that it can be taken directly where the medicine is needed, that is under the tongue as well as in the ear. It may also, when diluted with salt water, be taken as a gavage, although it is a bit grainy. If used as a gavage, rinse with pure salt water.

Treatment protocol

Take wild, raw chaga mushroom emulsion, about 40 drops under the tongue three times daily. Also, drip this into the involved ear(s). For a gavage add 40 drops to a glass of salt water and draw deeply into the sinus cavities. Repeat as needed and follow with a salt water rinse. Also, take the oil of wild oregano, five drops under the tongue several times daily. The oil may also be rubbed about the ear. A drop or two may be placed in the outer part of the ear canal. Additionally, use a wild oregano oil and sage oil-based sinus spray in a sea salt solution. For this merely lie on the back and squirt in a goodly amount. Repeat as needed. Chronic otitis media is usually due to fungal infection, and the combination of chaga mushroom and oregano oil reverses this.

Bronchitis

Traditionally in eastern Europe chaga is used to treat this disorder. The fact that this mushroom is effective against bronchitis is supported by a considerable amount of science. Chaga is highly antifungal, and bronchitis is largely a fungal disease. Tissue scrapings of people with bronchitis yield primarily fungi and only more rarely bacteria.

Chaga mushroom also possesses antiinflammatory powers, which make it invaluable in the treatment of chronic lung disorders. Furthermore, the fungal infections of bronchitis are deeply entrenched. Typically, in chronic bronchitis there are several fungi which invade and infect the bronchial tubes. Thus, there is a need to boost the immune response against these fungi, and this is precisely what chaga achieves.

In eastern Europe a hot water infusion of chaga is often the treatment of choice for this condition. Furthermore, such an infusion is effective in the prevention of this condition, since it acts in general to boost immune function.

Oil of oregano (wild, Mediterranean-source) is also a potent treatment for this condition. It aggressively destroys the fungi, which perpetrates this disease.

Treatment protocol

For chronic bronchitis take the emulsified spice oil-infused chaga mushroom extract, twenty drops under the tongue three or more times daily. Also, take Mediterranean source oil of wild oregano (wild hand-picked), five drops under the tongue twice daily. For tough cases also consume the wild oregano juice, an ounce daily. Additionally, drink birch bark-fortified wild chaga expresso, one or two cups daily. For acute infection double or triple these amounts.

Epstein-Barr virus

In many ways the Epstein-Barr virus is similar to the hepatitis C virus and even the AIDS virus. It often causes great wasting and destruction. Infection by this virus is a major cause of chronic fatigue syndrome. There are no known drugs, which kill the Epstein-Barr virus.

Chaga is highly active against this virus, as is birch bark. The chaga emulsion helps reverse Epstein-Barr by activation of the immune response. To accelerate the cure the liver must be purged, as this organ usually houses the virus. Here, wild, raw triple greens purging drops is ideal, as is the total body purging agent based upon raw, crude monounsaturated oils of black seed and extra virgin olive oil, with wild, raw greens and spice oils. This purging agent, made with raw, wild dandelion, burdock, and nettle, gives the most productive results when taken with meals rich in fats.

Treatment protocol

Take the emulsified spice oil-infused chaga mushroom extract, forty drops under the tongue three or more times daily. Also, take Mediterranean source oil of wild oregano (wild hand-picked), five drops under the tongue four times daily. Eat plenty of radishes and turnips. Also, eat raw onions daily. Additionally, take the wild-source body purging system, consisting of wild raw forest greens in a base of organic extra virgin olive oil, black seed oil, and raw apple cider vinegar, about an ounce twice daily, along with the triple greens flushing agent taken as drops under the tongue, about 40 drops twice daily. In tough cases the purge is essential for rooting out the viruses from the deepest recesses of the liver. For active/acute infection also take a natural-source vitamin C supplement consisting of wild raw camu camu and acerola cherry, two capsules twice daily. To bolster immunoglobulin production cold-fermented burbot oil, rich in vitamins A, D, and K, would be ideal, about a half teaspoon daily. This should be sufficient to achieve eradication.

Influenza, including swine flu

Seemingly, the flu is a cause of great consternation among humans. Constantly, the popular press broadcasts the potential and real threat of this illness. While its threat may be overstated that doesn't diminish its power. The flu virus is a killer. Furthermore, all people should attempt to avoid getting this condition, because even though it kills only rarely it may devastate a person's health.

Chaga extract is an essential treatment for this condition. This is because this extract activates a normal immune response. It is also because the flu is dangerous, and there is no guarantee that the immune system will halt it. The chaga boosts the overall immune response against the virus, and thus prevents serious consequences.

For flu birch bark extracts are also exceedingly potent. The tree bark flavonoids and proanthocyanidins, as well as the various bark sterols, are highly active against this virus.

Oil of wild oregano is another key natural cure against this infection. The government refuses to tell people about it, but the fact is wild oregano oil devastates this virus. Another key substance is fresh water co d liver oil, that is burbot liver oil, which is cold-fermented.

Treatment protocol

Take super-strength oil of wild oregano, several drops under the tongue as often as possible; this may be taken even every half hour or fifteen minutes. Also, take raw, wild emulsified chaga drops, 20 or more drops under the tongue repeatedly. Additionally, drink the wild chaga/birch bark expresso, several cups daily. For tough cases also consume the juice of oregano, an ounce repeatedly as well as the dessicated multiple spice oil capsules, two capsules repeatedly. Another forest cure, which is effective, is the wild, raw triple greens flushing agent, about 20 drops under the tongue four times daily. This is sufficient to cure the flu in most cases.

In tough cases it may be necessary to be even more aggressive. For resistant cases take the oil of oregano in a super-strength form, 20 to 40 drops under the tongue repeatedly, along with the multiple spice capsules containing dessicated oils of oregano, cinnamon, sage, and cumin, three capsules every hour or even every half hour (with juice or food, if necessary). Also, the chaga dose may be increased to two or three droppersful every half hour or hour. Additionally, the wild, raw berries extract can be taken, about forty drops every half hour or hour (available as a two-ounce bottle containing extracts from eight northern Canadian berries). As well, wild-source vitamin C can be consumed as wild, raw camu camu, ideally with acerola, two capsules every hour. Additionally, take cold-fermented burbot liver oil, the type rich in natural-source vitamins A, D, and K, about a teaspoon daily and then as maintenance a half teaspoon daily. Another option is wild sockeye salmon oil made from the heads of the fish, about a teaspoon or two daily.

For throat components use a wild cranberry- or cherry-based throat spray with wild cherry bark extract in a base of raw, wild honey: spray on the back of the throat as needed. This is a potent yet tasty cough therapy, which is also highly effective against sore throat, laryngitis, and tonsillitis.

Stomach and duodenal ulcers

Chaga has a prolonged use in the reversal of these disorders. The action of this mushroom is largely the result of its rich content of oxygenated substances, such as the sterols and SOD, which induce healing in the stomach and intestinal linings. Because of its antiinflammatory, germicidal, and wound healing properties poplar bud extract also exhibits a significant curative effect directly on the mucous membranes of the stomach. Plus, the raw apple cider vinegar has its own action, stimulating the healthy flow of digestive juices. In addition, vinegar has a tonic action on the stomach walls, in other words, it strengthens them.

Regarding chaga the spice oil emulsion is ideal. This is because it contains a number of substances which are anti-ulcer. Its use in the form of sublingual drops is highly activating and also gentle for the healing process. There is the chaga itself, which induces healing and also stimulates the local immune response. Note: more on this will be described in the chapter Systems Power.

Treatment protocol

Take the spice oil/extra virgin olive oil chaga emulsion, forty drops on an empty stomach three times daily. Also, take the wild raw poplar bud emulsion in a base of raw apple cider vinegar, 40 drops twice daily. Additionally, take Mediterranean-source oil of wild oregano (wild hand-picked), five drops under the tongue three times daily. This is sufficient to eradicate the ulcer. As well, take the whole crude wild oregano herb (with *Rhus coriaria*), two or more capsules twice daily. Also, make and drink raw cabbage juice, about eight ounces twice daily. Additionally, drink as the preferred beverage the wild high mountain oregano tea, one cup several times daily.

Fibromyalgia

This condition is largely an infectious disease. The infectious agents include difficult-to-detect microbes such as mycolplasmas, yeasts, molds, rusts, and spirochetes. Amebas and other parasites may also be involved.

Nicholson and his group have repeatedly shown that this disease is caused by infection. Through extensive investigation it was found that people with this condition are heavily infected by a wide range of pathogens, including mycoplasmas, chlamydia, coxiella, brucella, and the spirochete borrelia. Notes Nicholson in his article published in the Institute of Molecular Medicine people with this condition often suffer from a multiplicity of infections by such agents and possibly others unknown. The pathogens, says this investigator, were actually found in the peoples' blood. He says:

> In our recent study on CFS (chronic fatigue syndrome) and FMS (fibromyalgia syndrome) patients, most patients had multiple bacterial infections, especially if they had been sick for many years or had severe signs and symptoms.

He then describes an ominous finding, which demonstrates the degree of destruction caused by these germs:

> These infections invade the vascular system and cause coagulation problems, and they can cause or increase the risk of coronary diseases such as endocarditis and myocarditis.

Endocarditis and myocarditis are serious infections of the heart, the former affecting primarily the heart values and the latter the heart muscle. Obviously, untreated such infections are highly disastrous and may lead to not only disability but also premature death. In particular, Gulf War Syndrome victims are highly vulnerable to the development of such cardiovascular consequences.

Forest cures are the key to resolving this condition. The major ones are the wild oregano, particularly the whole crushed herb, along with the malic acid-rich *Rhus coriaria*, the chaga mushroom extract, the poplar bud extract, and the wild, raw berries extract.

The inflammation is due to the infection. Once the infection is purged the inflammation recedes. The infectious agents are aggressive and infect the system chronically. In inflammation the immune system is largely neutralized. It takes a major effort to purge such germs from the body.

Many fibromyalgia suffers are victims of vaccine injury. The vaccines introduce vile germs, which become established in the tissues. They also introduce a wide range of noxious chemicals directly into the bloodstream such as formaldehyde, mercury, aluminum, aspartame, and MSG. There is no reason to take such injections, and the consequences for the repeated use of vaccines is dire. One such consequence is fibromyalgia and similar inflammatory disorders.

Treatment protocol

Take the spice oil/extra virgin olive oil chaga emulsion, forty drops under the tongue two or three times daily. Take also the chaga/birch bark expresso, one or more cups daily. Additionally, take the wild, raw poplar bud emulsion in a base of raw apple cider vinegar, 40 or more drops twice daily. Crude whole wild oregano with *Rhus coriaria* (in capsules) is another forest medicine and is ideal for this condition: take three capsules twice daily with a full meal. The Mediterranean-source oil of wild oregano (wild hand-picked, mountain-grown) is a potent antimicrobial and antiinflammatory agent, five drops under the tongue twice daily. In severe cases enzymes may be required, notably bromelain and papain. Take a capsule combining these, two or more capsules twice daily. Also, extract of wild, raw poplar buds is a potent cure: take 40 or more drops twice daily as sublingual drops. Additionally, take the dessicated multiple spice capsules, two or more capsules three times daily.

Too, wild berries are also a top source of malic acid and other energizing compounds for the muscular tissues (see the book *The Wild Berry Cure*, Knowledge House Publishers, same author). Surely, wild, raw berries should be consumed. Or, take the wild, raw multiple berry extract, a potent nutritional supplement for this condition, as sublingual drops made from eight wild-source Canadian berries, 40 or more drops under the tongue twice daily. There is also the powerful wild, raw cherry extract made from remote-source chokecherries (known as Cherinol), 40 drops twice daily.

Chronic fatigue syndrome

This is the ideal condition, which responds to forest cures, particularly the chaga. Like fibromyalgia this condition is largely the result of massive infectious overload. Again, vaccine contamination is the usual culprit. The overuse of antibiotics can also result in the condition. This is because these drugs lead to fungal infection, and the fungi secrete poisons which corrupt the immune system as well as the musculoskeletal system. When such infectious agents are destroyed, the fatigue is eliminated.

In chronic fatigue syndrome there is usually dysfunction of the adrenal glands. These glands are involved in the energy mechanisms of the body. When the adrenal function fails, fatigue usually strikes, particularly in a certain pattern. That pattern is constant exhaustion, often unrelieved by rest. In contrast, with weak thyroid function the fatigue is in the morning, with an increase in energy as the day continues. In the case of adrenal collapse the fatigue is usually worse in the afternoon and evening. The adrenals produce steroids, and these steroids are needed for the maintenance of the blood sugar. So, much of the fatigue in people with adrenal weakness relates to low or imbalanced blood sugar. Of note, both the muscles and the brain are reliant on sugar in the form of blood glucose for their energy needs. Thus, in order for the normal mental and physical energy to be reestablished adrenal function must be normalized. For more information on this see *The Body Shape Diet* (Knowledge House Publishers, same author).

Regardless, the adrenal glands are greatly bolstered by steroid-rich forest medicine, notably emulsions of birch bark and chaga mushroom. Royal jelly is another potent natural medicine for regulating these glands, because this, too, is rich in highly nourishing substances, notably steroids and amino acids as well as the key adrenal-boosting vitamin pantothenic acid.

Treatment protocol

Take the spice oil/extra virgin olive oil chaga emulsion, forty drops under the tongue two or three times daily. Take also the chaga/birch bark expresso, one or more cups daily. Crude whole wild oregano with *Rhus coriaria* (in capsules) is ideal for this condition: take two capsules twice daily with or without food. The Mediterranean-source oil of wild oregano (wild hand-picked, mountain-grown) is a potent antimicrobial and antiinflammatory agent, five drops under the tongue twice daily. Wild, raw berries extracts are potent means for energizing the body. Take the wild and remote-source eight Canadian berries extract, as sublingual drops, 40 drops twice daily.

Again, for the adrenal glands the chaga extract is a potent medicine. So is undiluted royal jelly, particularly when combined with wild rosemary and sage. Take an undiluted royal jelly capsule (with ground rosemary and sage), four capsules every morning. Also, take crude royal jelly paste, either as an emulsion in Austrian pumpkinseed oil or in the regular form, a half teaspoonful daily. Furthermore, increase the consumption of sea salt, and eliminate the consumption of refined sugar, the latter being highly toxic to the adrenal glands.

Case histories: serious proof

Peoples' testimonies are far more critical than may be commonly realized. When a physician observes a response—when he/she records a positive benefit, particularly in the event of a disease that is non-responsive to other therapies—this is a major issue. It is an issue which should be recorded and published. Medical professionals often belittle testimonials as unscientific or even unreliable. Yet, incredibly, in its original era modern medicine was dependent upon testimonials through case histories, which are, essentially, human testimonies. Regardless, the fact that people benefit from the use of forest cures can never be taken lightly. In contrast to medical dogma case histories are invaluable. There is a caveat. They must be real case histories, not mere fabrications.

Here, real case histories are provided of measurable human results. These are people with resistant health challenges, which responded to forest cure therapy. Most of these case histories involve chaga:

Man with chronic neck pain described as a knot in the neck gains massive relief through whole food chaga extract:

Mr. P., a 54-year-old, suffered from a relentless neck disorder manifested by stiffness and tightness in the middle of his neck. He tried a number of supplements plus exercise for only modest relief. Then, he drank chaga-birch bark expresso. Within an hour he noticed a major improvement in his neck, with the knot-like region becoming supple. Within 24 hours nearly all the neck tightness had disappeared, which he regarded as a miracle. The chaga proved to be far more effective and far more lasting for this lesion than exercise. When he went a few days without the chaga the neck disorder returned, but in a diminished way. By taking the chaga daily or every other day the neck condition improved by some 90%. Moreover, for Mr. P. this was a chronic condition, which he had suffered with for over 10 years. This was a stupendous result.

With chaga expresso energy patterns change dramatically; less sleep required:

Mr. K. is a writer and educator, who also runs a large business. He prides himself on rising early and working while the rest of the world sleeps. However, for over two years he had been unable to do so, despite being in relatively good health. He began taking the chaga and birch bark expresso. Within 48 hours he noticed a major change in his pattern. Instead of arising at 6:30 a.m. and then collapsing back in bed he was able to arise at 5:30 a.m. then stay up, working the entire day. Thus, one issue was obvious to Mr. K., which is the fact that chaga creates massive changes in the body, which allows a person to function on a superior level. Mr. K. has now increased his workload significantly, not because of motivation but instead exclusively because of the intake of this potent cure.

On the first cup of chaga expresso yard maintenance expert works all day without the desire for food:

Mr. V. is a landscape maintenance manager. He works long hours, which includes heavy labor. So for 'energy' he starts his day with a large cup of coffee, without breakfast. He was given chaga/birch bark expresso by his boss. After his first cup he noticed something astounding. He was able to work vigorously until 6:00 p.m. without any desire for food. This, he said, he had never done previously in some 30 years, which he attributed exclusively to his cup of chaga expresso.

Man with morning grogginess eliminates mental fog with wild, raw chaga drops:

Mr. D. is a 55-year-old business owner with a history of sluggishness in the morning. Also a writer he had the desire to do much writing in the morning but often found this difficult. To combat this he began taking the emulsified chaga drops. Quickly, he noticed an increase in stamina and concentration and was able to write freely, without fatigue. Also, as a result of taking the chaga drops under the tongue his morning grogginess disappeared. This was effective even if taken the night before. If any mental fatigue occurred during his work, he would treat this by taking additional chaga drops under the tongue. There was a side effect, which was increased concentration throughout the day, including when driving.

Long-haul drivers suffer no fatigue despite a difficult journey on the chaga extract:

Mr. S., Mr. C, and Mr. D. had to make a 10-hour drive using people carriers. This was to get their clients to a distant airport before their flights. This include a considerable amount of night driving. Normally, they would tire easily and have to take breaks. By drinking the chaga tea/expresso and using the drops under the tongue there was pure energy, and, thus, they took no breaks. Their alertness, they said, was astounding and beyond expectations.

Chapter Six

Cancer Cures

Regarding cancer with the exception of orthodox therapies the cure word has been virtually banned. This is strictly because of financial interests. In the United States the medical monopoly seeks to crush all competition. This is particularly true of the marketing of any natural substances with known anticancer activity. Furthermore, since the early 1900s the medical monopolists have done this consistently, greatly reducing the possible choices for alternative approaches.

Yet, for example, there are numerous alternatives to poisonous chemicals and radiation. For instance, no one can dispute the power of chaga mushroom and birch bark in the destruction of cancer. Nor can anyone doubt the heavily researched role of wild, raw berry extracts as potent antitumor agents. Nor can the power of natural purging agents made from wild greens and heavy oils be disputed. Nor can anyone legitimately deny the powers of wild spice oils in the destruction of cancer cells. Thus, the information on these cures will be provided here, and let the people do with it what they may. They have a right to seek their own way. That is the native right of any human being—and despite the monopolists that is the way God made it.

Mechanism of action

This is always of interest to any cancer researcher. Even so, the mechanism of action of forest medicines is simple. These potent cures have the unique attribute of programming cancer cells to self destruct. They also protect healthy cells from the typical corruptions which lead to cancer.

With chaga mushroom there is especially significant documentation. In 1998 Polish investigators determined the precise anticancer action. Publishing in the Polish journal transcribed as accurately as possible as Bulletin of Chemistry and Pharmacy they found that chaga directly attacks tumors. It causes dramatic changes in the cancer cells' biology, particularly related to their growth. Ultimately, because of these actions the cancer cells stop growing and then implode. Additionally, a variety of investigators have shown that chaga is a potent antioxidant. The antioxidant power of this mushroom largely accounts for its role in the prevention of aging as well as many of its medical properties. For instance, Akiko found that it is such a powerful antioxidant that in test models it blocks genetic damage, known as antimutagenic effects. In other words, with the regular intake of chaga the gene substance can be preserved. Any substance which protects and preserves the genes increases lifespan.

As mentioned previously one of the key active ingredients of chaga and birch bark, betulin, is highly antitumor. Noda and his group discovered that this substance, found in rich supplies in birch bark as well as chaga, is specific to tumor cells. The tumor cells, they observed, have a different pH than the healthy cells. At this pH, incredibly, betulin is most active. The same is true of another key active ingredient of birch bark and chaga, which is betulininc acid. Fulda and colleagues determined (1997) that this substance causes cancer cells to self-destruct. This is the safest and most effective mechanism possible for anticancer agents.

Another forest cure, wild, raw berries and their extracts, also exert this effect. The extracts are particularly medicinal and have significant antitumor properties. It was Stoner and his group at Ohio State University who made many of the findings, in particular, regarding the highly potent black raspberry. Here, he determined, there is definite action against a wide range of cancers. The potency of this berry can be trapped through cold-processing, that is of the wild remote-source material growing away from human intervention. This is available in a two-ounce bottle as drops under the tongue.

For chaga another mechanism of action relates to SOD. This enzyme halts noxious reactions involving oxygen, which lead to gene damage. Then, too, it is such gene damage which is largely responsible for both aging and the onset of degenerative disease. Any substance which stalls gene damage is highly beneficial to the body. Thus, the regular intake of SOD-rich chaga emulsion, as well as the infusion/expresso with wild birch bark and purple maca, is an efficient means to stall the aging process.

The polysaccharides in chaga offer yet another mechanism of action. As described previously, like chaga's sterols this is responsible for activating the natural immune response, including the native response against tumors. So, with such vast powers—the sterols, SOD, and polysaccharides—it is no wonder that the results of chaga supplementation have been deemed virtually miraculous. All these elements operate through the same mechanism of action, which is to induce programmed cell death, that is apoptosis, in diseased cells.

Birch bark: potent tree medicine

While birch bark has already been mentioned it is helpful to emphasize the nature of its properties. The chaga gets all its power from the birch tree. Thus, the tree itself is medicinal. This is particularly true of the bark. Both the outer and inner bark have been used medicinally.

The bark is rich in a key compound, known as betulin. A derivative of this, betulinic acid, is the subject of extensive cancer research. The bark compounds are the subject of extensive research, particularly related to potent anticancer actions. This began with a study done in 1995 by University of Chicago-Illinois' John Pezzuto. As reported in the *San Francisco Chronicle* Pezzuto found that the peeling white bark of the birch tree has the ability to shrink melanoma cancers. In his study in mice he determined that regarding its ability to destroy melanoma cells the birch bark extract was superior to any drug.

The researchers put melanoma cells under the skin of mice. Once tumors developed the animals received six doses of the birch bark extract by injection. As a result of this treatment there was a major shrinkage of the tumors, up to 70%. In some cases the tumors virtually disappeared. Yet, there was an even more spectacular result, which is prevention. Incredibly, in some mice, which were given the birch bark components simultaneously with the cancer cells, no melanoma tumors developed. No wonder birch trees can withstand the glaring hot sun of the northern climate, as well as the fierce cold, without being damaged.

Since Pezzuto's original research there have been hundreds of articles published on birch bark or, more specifically, betulinic acid, one of its components. While betulinic acid is powerful. It is only one of hundreds of substances found in the bark. Historically, it is well known that the action of isolates is inferior compared to the whole unprocessed substance. Betulinic acid, that is the type used in the research, is actually an altered form of the main active ingredient of birch bark, which is betulin.

Both betulin and betulinic acid have antitumor properties. In research studies the acid form is the type most commonly used, and no studies are being currently done comparing the whole crude bark versus a mere isolate. This is because the objective is to turn betulinic acid into a patented drug.

There is no need for this. The whole crude bark is an ideal medicine and is, in fact, superior to any isolate. This is particularly true of the remote-source material. An ideal birch bark supplement combines both the outer and inner bark cold-pulverized into as fine of a powder as possible. As a powdered tea this is ideally consumed along with a natural source of cholesterol such as royal jelly powder, yolk of organic egg, whole organic yogurt, or whole milk solids. The combination of plant steroids with animal steroids, that is cholesterol, greatly increases the potency. This is particularly true when combating diseases of the nervous system, especially cancer of the brain and neurological tissues as well as multiple sclerosis, Alzheimer's disease, Parkinson's disease, and ALS. Another form is to take birch bark as emulsified liquid drops under the tongue. There is also wild white birch bark tea with organic maca.

With any natural medicine the whole food form is always preferable. This is what the animals consume, and their vitality is obvious. Thus, with chaga and birch bark supplements seek those companies which make the least crude unprocessed yet potent extract possible.

This use of the whole substance is the true history of natural medicine. Too, the natives relied upon natural medicines, as well as wild foods, in their whole form. They had never fragmented their medicine into parts but, rather, consumed them in their entirety. To reiterate with the patented extract, for instance, the betulinic acid, this is produced through much refinement. Moreover, the method used for the refinement is so-called fractional distillation. Then, the substance is extracted from the whole using a highly poisonous solvent, known as methanol. This solvent is also known as wood alcohol. Even in insignificant amounts wood alcohol is highly toxic, causing blindness and even fatality. A special process must be used to remove residues of this toxin. Treating an herb/plant with such a poison always causes corruption. At a minimum it reduces the biological activity of the molecules. Likewise, mere ethyl alcohol also does this. Thus, regarding concentrates of chaga it is the non-alcoholic extracts, such as the chaga emulsion and infusion/expresso, which are most desirable. There is no way to make a powerful/safe medicine through the ingestion of poisons. That is why rather than chemically extracted isolates the whole substance must be used. The wild chaga expresso, wild, raw emulsified chaga drops, birch bark tea, and the birch bark emulsion are true whole food supplements made without the use of any sort of harsh or noxious chemical.

Whole crude ground birch bark is a component of wild chaga mushroom drops. This creates a significant synergy with the mushroom. The extraction/emulsification process, which is proprietory, is free of all chemicals, renders the normally difficult to absorb fatty sterols absorbable. This is a unique advantage only offered by the emulsified cinnamon-tasting drops.

Again, this emulsification causes the sterols to mix in water, like a natural soap, in other words, now the steroid substances can be quickly absorbed, so they can perform their critical functions. Otherwise, these waxes are largely lost. Think about it. Normally, waxes are highly resistant to water. That is why they are so useful, like the wax applied to a car. The components of tree mushrooms are similar. The waxes serve the function to prevent the fungi from becoming water-logged.

Intuitively, the Siberian villagers realized this, finding that the best way to consume chaga, was as a hot infusion. They would boil a small amount in a liter of water for up to two hours. Then, they would add more water, and re-boil it. This water-upon-water treatment is precisely correct, since this causes the sterols to become super-saturated in the hot water. In other words, this hot water method causes the sterols to be dissolved into solution and, thus, the water becomes saturated with them. With the chaga-birch bark expresso the simplest method for extraction is to merely put a teaspoon or less in a cup of boiling water and, then, allow it to sit without refrigeration for at least 48 hours. This is superior to the commercial method of repeated boiling. Although some of the active ingredients are concentrated through this method the enzymes are destroyed.

There is also the emulsified version, which contains the spice oils of wild oregano and clove. These spice oils improve the absorption of the chaga components. Moreover, like chaga, spice oils are germicidal and antifungal. Furthermore, spice oils help prevent the mushroom extract from oxidizing. This emulsification may be noticed by a creamy-colored material inside the dropper tube. This is merely the extraction of natural waxes and sterols, which cling slightly to the glass.

Additionally, wild birch bark is available pulverized as a component of the chaga expresso and also separately. Again, these are mixed in just boiled water. Then, they should be allowed to steep for a few minutes, and drunk plain or with honey. Ideally, it should be consumed with whole organic milk, since the steroids in milk increase the activity of the key ingredients. Milk fat also helps emulsify the chaga and birch bark sterols. Or, it may be added to a blender with an organic egg yolk. Another option is to drink the hot tea when eating fatty animal foods. In the event of allergies to such foods almond or rice milk is an alternative.

Even so, surely, extracts of barks are far safer in cancer treatment than synthetic chemicals. The research is proving that such extracts destroy cancer cells, while never destroying the patient. Nor do the forest medicines, such as birch bark concentrates, poplar bud extract, and chaga mushroom, cause even the slightest degree of organ damage. Rather, they protect the organs from such damage. Regardless, this is a tremendous feat, that the medicine is powerful enough to kill tumors while completely gentle to healthy cells. In other words, such medicines block the processes that lead to inflammation and cancer but never impede those life processes of normal function. Rather, the forest cures mentioned in this book enhance such life processes. So, let us review the specific scientific studies of how birch bark and its components offer real hope for those suffering with degenerative and deadly diseases.

Blood cancer (sarcoma)

Some cancers spread through invasion of local tissues, while others are mainly blood-born. The latter are known as sacroma lesions. Leukemia is a sarcoma. A sarcoma may also be known as a blood cancer. These cancers are essentially diseases of the connective tissues. Thus, cancers of the bone and bone marrow are sarcomas—and this explains why leukemia is a sarcoma.

In any such cancer chaga is an ideal medicine. So is wild birch bark. Poplar bud extract is also active against blood-borne infections, as are the various wild, raw berry extracts, particularly extracts of lingonberry, blackberry, and black raspberry. All such extracts should be consumed in the battle against sacroma-type cancers. These are available as sublingual drops.

Treatment protocol

Take the chaga mushroom emulsion, 100 drops twice daily. Take also the wild birch bark emulsion, 100 drops twice daily. In addition, take the wild, raw poplar bud emulsion, 100 drops twice daily as well as the various wild, raw berry extracts as sublingual drops, that is drops of wild black raspberry, blackberry, and lingonberry, 40 drops of each three times daily. Additionally, take oil of wild oregano, 10 or more drops twice daily. Note: these specially prepared raw drops are relatively rare and are available in limited supplies. Look for two-ounce bottles containing such raw materials for use as sublingual drops.

Melanoma

With melanoma a major discovery has been made. This is the fact that mere forest cures, such as the betulin and betulinic acid of birch bark and chaga mushroom, kill melanoma cells. In a landmark finding tests show that human melanoma cells in tissue culture are readily destroyed by birch extract. Regardless, this should be no surprise, since a significant number of anti-cancer drugs are derived from natural products. Chaga is perhaps one of the most powerful of these, because even in a crude, natural form it halts the growth of cancer cells, including the cells of melanoma.

Again, the original work was done in Chicago by John Pezzuto, who showed that the birch component specifically targeted melanoma cells, causing them to die. This was followed by another study seeking the mechanism of action of white birch bark. The researchers discovered that the birch extract caused "programmed cell death in human melanoma cells." This is a stupendous finding. It means that the cancer cells essentially imploded. It was found that the birch bark substance, in this case betulinic acid, changed the electrical chemistry within the cancer cells, specifically at the level of the mitochondria. Also, the enzyme activities were altered, with enzymes which cause cancer cell death to be activated. Betulinic acid acted directly on the cancer cell membranes, weakening them and, thus, inducing self-destruction.

Studies in mice confirm the effects. Here, mice which are vulnerable to developing melanoma were injected with the cancerous cells. Tumor size was observed for 40 days following the injections of the birch extract (betulinic acid). This birch extract blocked tumor growth, and there was no toxicity nor any side effects. Here, the researchers specifically looked for evidence of drug toxicity, such as weight loss and sluggishness, but couldn't find any.

What the researchers have proven is impressive. This is the fact that forest cures, such as extracts or concentrates of birch bark, are far more powerful as anticancer agents than even the most potent drugs known. Betulinic acid alone proved superior to the most powerful chemotherapeutic drugs, including cataphoretic, Mithratic A, Eucosmidae, vinblastine, and vincristine, by over 50%, without causing toxicity such as bone marrow destruction, heart muscle damage, kidney damage, and destruction of the immune system. On the contrary birch bark and its extracts enhance the functions of these organs and organ systems.

The mechanism of action for betulinic acid is to a degree known. It would appear that this compound creates a systematic destruction of melanoma cells. It is as if betulinic acid and/or birch bark extract is 'programmed' for killing these cells.

Here is the point. Birch molecules store molecular energy. This is in the form of photonic energy from the sun. When the birch compounds are consumed, these energy molecules are released. These birch molecules change the electricity of the cancer cells, that since their polarity is changed the cancer cells die. It is well known that cancer is a disease related to pH. Inside the tumor cell an acidic environment develops.

Birch components are most active in an acidic environment. This is a kind of miracle, which should cause people to consider the concentrated power of wild nature.

The Japanese have also investigated the powers of birch against this disease. As published in the *British Journal of Cancer* birch extract increased the antitumor power against melanoma of the potent chemotherapy drug vincristine. This means that the birch compounds are themselves chemotherapeutic agents but are non-toxic in contrast to the standard ones commonly used. Regardless, there is no need to isolate any one compound from the bark. The whole crude bark extract from remote-source trees is sufficiently powerful as a synergistic complex. Moreover, a whole food chaga extract, combined with whole remote-source birch bark, is the ideal supplement, since these two forest cures work synergistically.

Treatment protocol

Use super/high strength oil of oregano topically on any lesion. Do this repeatedly. Add drops of wild, raw eight berries extract and/or wild, raw black raspberry extract. Also, add drops of wild, raw emulsion of chaga. Additionally, take the chaga emulsion, 50 drops three times daily, as well as the birch bark emulsion, 100 drops three times daily. Take also the wild, raw eight berries drops, 100 drops twice daily, along with the wild, raw black raspberry extract, 100 drops twice daily. Also, take juices of wild oregano and rosemary, an ounce of each twice daily. Furthermore, use the birch bark drops topically. Saturate a gauze pad and apply. Repeat as needed.

Brain cancer

For modern medicine there is little hope for this condition. The treatments are usually more noxious than the disease.

There is much evidence that the typical approach, radiation, surgery, and chemotherapy, is fraudulent. This is because brain cancer is often caused by a fault in the immune system. It is also frequently the result of actual infection of the brain. Furthermore, it may be directly caused by radiation. Then, should a person take radiation for a disease which this process actually induces?

With such a hopeless approach, no doubt, the power of natural medicines must be realized. Clearly, in the fight against brain cancer, natural medicines are invaluable. Perhaps the most potent of these are those medicines rich in betulin and betulinic acid, that is wild birch bark and chaga.

As mentioned previously these mushroom- and bark-source medicines have been shown to cause programmed cell death in tumor cells. In a cell culture trial betulinic acid, a key birch bark and chaga mushroom component, has been tested. This was against a kind of brain tumor known as glioblastoma, which is the most malignant of all types. The average survival time after this tumor has been diagnosed is a mere year. This, of course, is under conventional therapy. In this trial, the results of which are published in *Acta Neurochirurgica*, birch bark extract was tested against standard therapies, which include chemotherapeutic drugs and radiation. It was found that birch bark extract was more effective than all such drugs/therapies, the extract (betulinic acid) being over twice as powerful as the standard chemical cocktail and some eight times more effective than radiation. Then, what did the birch component achieve? It was the selective destruction of glioblastoma brain tumor cells, while proving non-toxic to human cells. According to the investigators the action of birch extract as a destroyer of glioblastoma cells was "marked."

Fulda and his group publishing in *Cancer Research* made similar findings. Here, it was concluded that, specifically, betulinic acid "exhibited significant antitumor activity" on cells derived from patients with glioblastomas. One novel finding of this research was that the birch bark extract was more effective against resistant forms of the cancer than any drug. Even these researchers, conservative as they are, called this tree cure "promising for the treatment of (brain) tumors."

In 1999 Wick and colleagues at Germany's Tubingen School of Medicine also achieved impressive results. Here, it was demonstrated that this forest cure "triggers apoptosis in five human glioma cell lines." In other words, five different types of brain tumor cells succumbed to the tree bark extract's powers. Directly, the tree bark component caused the specific destruction of these rapidly-growing brain tumor cells. Somehow, in what is a true miracle of nature the component, betulinic acid, caused oxygen molecules to be generated which then caused the implosion of the cancer cells.

Some of the mechanisms of action were observed. This tree medicine performed a miraculous feat by activating key enzymes that cleave dangerous compounds in order to inactivate the malignant cells. These enzymes are known as caspases, and they serve to slice off a tumor cell activator known as poly-polymerase. This, then, causes a halt in tumor cell reproduction. Ultimately, note the researchers, the result is cancer cell death, all triggered exclusively by this powerful cure. These investigators even found that the birch bark derivative caused the production of new protein molecules the purpose of which was to shut down cancer cell growth. Also, in a virtually miraculous fashion powerful forms of oxygen were manufactured, which then set about disabling and ultimately destroying cancer cells.

Fulda also indicated the value of birch extracts in brain tumors of children, including glioblastoma, Ewing's sarcoma, neuroblastoma, and medulloblastoma. Birch therapy, he writes, caused brain cancer cells to self-destruct.

The birch treatment had a direct effect on the energy factories in the cancer cells, the mitochondria. Here, the birch therapy had a profound effect. It simply caused the mitochondria to fail in their ability to produce energy. Without such energy production the cancer cells wither and die. The birch bark compounds attack the tumorous mitochondria, causing them to implode. There can be no more astounding action than this, which is a testimony to the ultimate power of wild forest cures, particularly highly potent birch bark extracts.

Treatment protocol

Take the chaga emulsion, 100 drops under the tongue two or more times daily. Also, take the birch bark emulsion, 100 drops under the tongue twice daily. Take also the chaga/birch bark expresso, two or more cups daily. As well, consume wild, raw berries drops as sublingual drops, notably the extracts of raw lingonberry, blackberry, and black raspberry. Additionally, take juice of wild oregano and juice of wild rosemary, as these extracts cross the blood-brain barrier, An ounce or more twice daily is a minimum amount.

Liver disease

Chaga mushroom and also birch bark extract have highly positive actions on the liver. Never dangerous, they can only assist the function of this organ. There is no liver toxicity from the ingestion of these tree foods. Instead, chaga and birch extracts prevent liver damage, particularly the type of damage which results from the ingestion of noxious chemicals.

The protective effect on liver function was demonstrated by Korean investigators, who tested liver cells in culture, which were incubated with chaga extract. In liver cells there is a method of communication, where cells attempt to protect insults. This communication is [...]saging. While each cell is a [...]d through intracellular gaps. In [...]es are delivered through these [...] are produced which halt this [...]re soaking in a chaga solution. [...]ded, which blocks intracellular [...]bly, the chaga extract prevented [...]isruption. As long as the cells [...]icate, the cancer couldn't form. [...] to cell communication through [...]actor in the life and death balance of cells..." This is because the intracellular communication gaps have a key function in maintaining the balance of health, in keeping the physiological processes in tune, and in regulating the growth, as well as strategic death, of living cells. Thus, concluded the researchers, chaga mushroom may "act as a natural anticancer product" by keeping the intracellular communication intact and by blocking all enzymes, which disrupt this system.

In Korea chaga mushroom is a traditional and even modern medicine for cancer. Y. Myung-Ja and his group publishing in *World Journal of Gastroenterology* found rather remarkable effects of chaga extract, in this case against liver cancer cells. When the cancer cells were treated with the chaga extract the viability of these cells was "markedly reduced." Noted the investigators, "Chaga inhibited the growth in a dose-dependent manner…which was accompanied (by) apoptotic cell death." This means that as the dosage was increased there was an increased killing effect. Yet, when normal liver cells were treated, there was no action against these. This proves that as an antitumor agent chaga is infinitely safer than the orthodox drugs which not only kill tumor cells but also kill human ones, including the cells of the bone marrow and liver itself. In contrast, in a most impressive feat that only divinely-produced nature can achieve emulsified extracts of both chaga and birch bark, when they kill, only do so against all that is noxious—all that causes disease.

Treatment protocol

To purge the liver of germs take the wild, raw chaga mushroom drops, 40 drops twice daily. Also, drink the chaga/birch bark expresso, one cup daily. To purge the liver of toxic compounds take the total body purging agent, about an ounce daily or in severe cases two ounces daily. Do this for at least a month. Also, take the wild raw greens flush, 40 drops under the tongue twice daily. Consume extra virgin olive oil as often as possible, as well as oil of black seed (both of these are in the purging agent). Additionally, take the wild, raw purple maca drops, 20 to 40 drops twice daily.

Prostate cancer

Tree cures are invaluable for this condition. This is largely due to their rich content of sterols, that is those cures derived from bark or bark-growing mushrooms. At Texas A & M University birch bark extract was studied against prostate cancer cells. The investigators found that this tree cure aggressively halted the growth of these tumor cells. As a bonus the mechanism of action was largely discovered. Cancer thrives because of its aggression, this being the aggressive production of blood vessels. The investigators knew that chaga halted tumor growth. Could this have been through its effect on the wild-growing blood vessels, which supply tumors?

These massively produced blood vessels are necessary to create the vast blood supply of the tumor. Without the blood vessels the tumor dies. Enter the role of vascular endothelial growth factor (VEGF). This factor is produced by the tumors as a stimulant. The Texas investigators measured this as well as a protein made by tumor cells, which blocks their self-destruction. This protein, known descriptively as survivin, is a key to the maintenance of the cancer. The birch medicine acted on these proteins by, in fact, degrading them. This was achieved at the highest level possible, within the cell nucleus. Thus, the components of birch tree, as found both in the whole crude remote-source bark and the whole chaga mushroom, are a specific natural medicine against cancer. This is the nature of the divine system. It is realized that people are often appalled at the mention of this system. Yet, it bears repeating, which is that this is no accident, in other words, it is all by design. For the human race cures have been made in advance. It is only a matter of finding them.

Prostate tissues are highly vulnerable to this vascularization. Slowly, with this increased blood supply the tumor smolders, gradually impinging upon the urinary flow. Ultimately, obvious symptoms develop, but by this time the tumor may become established. The artificial blood supply feeds the cancer growth, and, thus, for the cure to be successful this system must be destroyed. Both chaga mushroom and the remote-source birch bark act directly on this by causing the collapse of the cancer's blood supply.

Oyster mushroom is specifically active against prostate cancer. This was demonstrated in a study in the *Journal of Medicinal Food* by Gu and Sivam, who documented how the mushroom extract caused rapid cell death (rapid apoptosis) of prostate cancer cells in tissue culture.

Other forest foods do so, in particular wild berries. One reason is their action on the blood supply to tumors. The flavonoids in berries are modulators of blood flow. A number of studies have demonstrated that these flavonoids, along with other active ingredients in berries known as polyphenols, also cause the destruction of the blood supply to tumors. The berries are active only in the raw state or freeze-dried.

Raw, wild berry extracts, which are made from hand-picked wild berries from the far northern forests, are now available. In particular, there is an eight wild berry extract available, which contains wild, raw extracts of chokecherry, blueberry, black raspberry, red raspberry, saskatoon berry, lingonberry, blackberry, and wild high bush cranberry. There is also a wild, raw sarsaparilla berry extract as well as a wild, raw brambleberry (blackberry) extract. Wild, raw lingonberry (two-ounce bottle, drops under the tongue) can also be found as a separate extract, and this is a potent natural medicine for prostate cancer. In the fight against cancer these extracts are ideal companions to the chaga mushroom/birch bark extracts. In addition, wild, raw poplar bud extract in a base of extra virgin olive oil and apple cider vinegar should be consumed, again as drops under the tongue (or internally in juice or water). Virtually no disease can resist the powers of these vital extracts—all made from the medicines of the far northern forests, where nature is still intact.

Treatment protocol

Take the chaga emulsion, 100 drops under the tongue two or more times daily. Also, take the birch bark emulsion, 100 drops under the tongue. Additionally, take high powered wild, raw berry extracts, specifically the wild lingonberry and black raspberry extracts, about 100 drops twice daily of each. The lingonberry is specifically powerful for the pelvic organs and is active against prostatic disease. Yet, so is raw black raspberry extract, which has a high antitumor activity.

Fungi are a major component of prostate cancer. These pathogens cause a vast amount of irritation. This may lead to the development of abnormal growths and ultimately tumor. This is why the fungi must be purged. This is through the intake of wild oil of oregano. Take 20 drops of a super-strong type of oil of wild oregano (wild hand-picked) twice daily, along with the juice of wild oregano, an ounce twice daily.

Colon cancer

This is the great plague of modern humans. Stool which remains in the colon for prolonged periods causes massive irritation. This may lead to cancer. Also, there are a number of substances in the Western diet which increase the risks for this disease, notably nitrated meats, pork, refined vegetable oil, hydrogenated vegetable oil, alcohol, white flour, white rice, artificial food dyes, and refined sugar. Additionally, a low intake of fruit and vegetables is a causative factor. The fibrous components of fruit and vegetables help keep the colon evacuated and, thus, block the development of bowel tumors.

Historically, chaga has been used for cancers of the gut, including colon cancer. The intestines contain a considerable amount of immune cells, which act as surveillance agents to capture and kill cancer cells. In fact, some 60% of the mass of all immune cells are located in the intestines, primarily in the lower small intestine. This region of cells in the small intestines is known as the Peyer's Patches. Chaga places these cells in a high state of readiness.

According to Korean investigators publishing in the *Journal of the Korean Society of Food Science and Nutrition* (2004) chaga is truly active against this disease. In the study chaga extract, in this case combined with powdered green tea, was tested against a human cancer cell strain as well as a stomach cancer cell strain. Noted the investigators the chaga extract exhibited "highly antiproliferative effect(s) in human colon cancer" cells and also human stomach cancer cells. This was through a process known as programmed cell death or apoptosis. In other words, chaga extract was directly poisonous to cancer cells. In contrast, there was no such action against normal cells, which were also tested as a part of the study.

One factor which must be considered in this disease is the role of parasites. Such invaders cause vast amounts of inflammation. As demonstrated by Hulda Clark, N. D., such a process is a major cause of colon cancer. The parasites may be found not only in the colon wall but also in the lungs and liver. One of the most significant of these is the human intestinal fluke or flukes from sheep, cows, and/or pigs. Thus, for the vigorous cure of this disease the intake of purging agents which cleanse and destroy such parasites is crucial.

Treatment protocol

For this disease the intake of all types of red meat should be halted. In particular , the consumption of nitrated meat and pork must be banned. For protein organic whole milk, cottage cheese, and yogurt may be consumed. Additionally, there must be no consumption of white flour, white rice, refined sugar, synthetic food dyes, corn syrup, and artificial flavors. MSG, synthetic food dyes, and aspartame must be banned. All are carcinogenic. All cause noxious reactions in the body that lead to inflammation as well as allergic shock.

To treat colon cancer it is important to increase the consumption of fruit and vegetables. A focus should be placed on organic and/or wild berries. In this regard if the berries are unavailable use potent wild forest cures, that is wild raw berries drops such as the eight wild, raw Canadian berries extract, wild, raw bramble (black) berry extract, and, particularly, the wild, raw black raspberry extract, as found in a two-ounce bottle. Also, wild raw lingonberry extract, as drops under the tongue, is highly antitumor and has been documented as effective against colon cancer: of each of these wild berries drops take 40 drops under the tongue twice daily. Also, take a wild, raw triple greens flushing agent, about 40 drops twice daily. Oil of remote-source fennel in an extra virgin olive oil base is also invaluable, particularly as an antiparasitic agent against hookworm, tapeworm, and flukes: take 40 drops twice daily.

Take a total body purging agent consisting of heavy cold-pressed monounsaturated oils of black seed and extra virgin olive, along with raw apple cider vinegar, wild, raw greens, and spice oils, about an ounce twice daily. Additionally, take wild, raw emulsified chaga extract, about 100 drops two or three times daily. As well, take emulsified raw, wild birch bark, 50 drops two or more times daily. Take also wild oregano juice, an ounce twice daily. Furthermore, the juice of wild oregano should be consumed, about an ounce twice daily. It is also important to eat plenty of turnips and radishes. These contain sulfur and selenium, which help kill colon cancer cells.

Uterine/cervical cancer

No doubt, forest extracts are generalized anticancer agents. This is true of the wild raw chaga mushroom extract, the wild raw poplar bud extract, and the wild raw berries extracts. Yet, in particular, in cancer chaga mushroom has universal effects. This is well established in Russia and eastern Europe, where chaga extracts have been used since the 1950s in the treatment of various cancers, including certain female cancers such as uterine, cervical, and breast tumors. In a study done by Polish investigators at the Silesian Medical Academy the destructive effects of chaga mushroom extract was evaluated against uterine cancer cells. There was a direct positive effect against the cancer cells as manifested by blockage of their growth, DNA disruption, and a reduction in cancer cell metabolic rate. All this was achieved through the use of a water extract of the mushroom similar to the one available as drops under the tongue or as an expresso.

Treatment protocol

To treat this condition all the powerful forest cures, the poplar bud extract, the chaga emulsion, the birch bark emulsion, and the wild, raw berry extract, along with the wild, raw lingonberry extract, should be used. The most potent wild berry extracts for the female system are the wild, raw raspberry, lingonberry, and black raspberry extracts. In addition, take the oil of wild oregano and the juice of wild oregano. Dosages vary, but regarding the drops at least 40 drops twice daily of all these various natural cures must consumed, ideally sublingually. Regarding the juice of oregano at least two ounces daily must be consumed, along with 20 or more drops twice daily of the oil of wild oregano.

Leukemia and lymphoma

To a degree leukemia was covered under the heading "Sarcoma." It must be reiterated that chaga mushroom, wild raw berries drops, wild raw greens drops, and wild raw poplar bark extract all have broad spectrum actions against cancer cells. Thus, regardless of the type of tumor it is expected that there would be a positive effect. Regarding chaga there was an early investigation which showed a profound action against, for instance, leukemia. As reported by Polish investigators chaga demonstrated a most potent action against vile leukemia cells. It simply digested them, particularly their cell nuclei. The investigators, publishing in the mid-1950s, Cracow, Poland, found that a compound in chaga "selectively digests the nuclei of chronic granulocytic leukemia" but then, the investigators noted, "it does not" harm healthy cells.

The investigators, led by J. Krauss-Zaki, could see this action of chaga on actual slides, which were smeared with the diseased cells. Apparently, this mushroom contains enzymes which specifically digest tumor cells. These enzymes are known as DNAase and RNAase. There could be no more powerful mechanism than this in the reversal of this life-threatening disease. Since these enzymes are disrupted by excess heat the ideal form of chaga for this condition is the raw, wild sublingual drops.

Cancer is highly susceptible to tree medicines, notably wild, raw birch bark, poplar bud, and chaga extracts. This is particularly true of leukemia. Another forest cure which is active against this disease is wild, raw berry extracts. The eight wild, raw berry extract, along with the wild, raw black raspberry extract, would be ideal for the systematic destruction of this cancer. Another significant antitumor berry extract is the wild, raw lingonberry extract. All these extracts are taken as drops under the tongue.

The combination of the birch bark, chaga, poplar bud, wild oregano juice, and wild berry extracts is sufficient to block the growth of any cancer, that is to prevent it from invading the internal organs. Then, through the aggressive intake of these powerful medicines the immune system can successfully purge the cancer from the body. Plus, these extracts themselves are directly antitumor.

Treatment protocol

Take the chaga emulsion, 100 drops under the tongue two or more times daily. Also, take the birch bark emulsion, 100 drops under tongue twice daily. Furthermore, consume the wild white birch bark tea, about two cups daily. Also, consume large amounts of wild oregano juice, about four ounces daily, along with the oil of wild oregano, 20 drops three times daily.

Wild, raw berries extracts are highly antitumor. To destroy these infectious cancers take wild, raw black raspberry extract, (rubus species) 50 drops twice daily as well as the wild, raw eight berries extract (northern Canadian wild berries), about 100 drops twice daily.

Chapter Seven

Systems Power

Trees operate via a system. They must maintain great strength to resist the elements. They must stand tall to survive. Life is all about attempting to destroy them. Yet, miraculously they thrive. This is largely the result of the potent biological chemicals synthesized by these miraculous beings. For humans the key is to gain the benefit of these powers through internal consumption. Let us look at all the ways chaga and birch bark extracts in particular and to a lesser degree all forest medicines impact the systems of the body.

Physical strength

It is difficult to imagine that there could be a more significant complex other than chaga for the creation of physical strength. No doubt, the infusion of the whole crude remote-source birch bark is also a source of much power. So is raw poplar buds made into an alcohol-free extract. All such tree extracts/concentrates are rich in sterols, and it is the sterols which give the human physical strength. The fact that they are rich in sterols is of immense significance. This is because these substances are precursors to the production of human hormones. Plus, they are, essentially, plant hormones. It is the hormones which are the most powerful of all bodily substances.

For athletic prowess of all natural substances hormones are the most desirable. In addition, since synthetic hormones are banned plant hormones are the ideal option. These hormones are powerful but safe. Plus, they have no interaction that might cause problems for professional athletes. For instance, the plant sterols do not show up in the blood or urine as banned substances. Despite this, they are equally as powerful if not more powerful than any synthetic hormones. Actually, they are considerably more powerful, because while synthetic hormones disrupt the physiology the natural hormones, as found in a balanced system in tree medicines, balance the body's mechanisms. There is great power in balance, and, perhaps, this is the key component of the medicinal properties of chaga and all other bark medicines. Regardless, what could be greater for gaining physical strength and balance than to consume the trapped energy of trees?

The beauty of the forest cures is that they work on the fatty membranes of the cells. This is precisely the region of action of the hormones (the hormones also work on the cell nucleus, but this, too, is fatty). Forest cures, particularly those from trees, are rich in sterols, because these membrane components are part of the architecture of the plant. For athletes this is critical, because sports places a certain amount of stress on the cellular components. Studies have shown that vigorous athletic activities, such as jogging, gymnastics, tennis, and racquetball, create toxic forms of oxygen. With strong membrane components and adequate supplies of vitamins and minerals these potentially dangerous molecules are rendered impotent. Antioxidants/nutrients needed to neutralize exercise-induced free radicals include vitamin C, vitamin E, pantothenic acid, niacin, riboflavin, and selenium. Radical forms of oxygen are also neutralized by plant flavonoids and phenolic compounds, which are found in rich amounts in forest cures, particularly the highly antioxidative wild poplar bud extract, the chaga/birch bark extract, and the wild raw berries extract. Furthermore, chaga and tree bark extracts offer the benefit of rich supplies of enzymes with potent antioxidant powers such as catalase and superoxide dismutase (SOD).

In addition, the steroids (sterols) are needed for withstanding athletic activity and also for recovery. The desire for exercise and/or vigorous sports is largely dependent upon these molecules. The forest medicines mentioned here provide a wide range of potent sterols, which are precursors to the manufacture of steroids in the human body. In nature these sterols, including betulin and betulinic acid, are responsible for maintaining the structure of powerful trees. They are also needed to protect the tree from disease. Then, their intake will do the same in humans, creating a powerful structure that is resistant to toxicity of daily living, reactive forms of oxygen, and harsh or vigorous exercise and the onset of diseases of degeneration. Other top sources of sterols/steroids include avocados, olives (and extra virgin olive oil), nuts, seeds, the flesh from grass-fed animals, organic poultry, fatty fish, whole milk products, natural eggs, and seafood. The top source of steroids is royal jelly (undiluted), which contains some six percent by weight.

Thus, through natural supplements the desire for exercise can be achieved. In addition, strength and stamina can be significantly increased. This is largely through the intake of key vitamins and minerals in a natural form as well as actual natural extracts which boost stamina such as wild, raw greens drops, wild, raw berries extracts, and chaga mushroom. The basic regimen for athletic prowess is as follows:

- emulsified royal jelly paste in a seed oil (pumpkinseed oil) base: take a half teaspoon twice daily
- undiluted royal jelly capsules with wild rosemary and sage: two or more capsules every morning
- natural-source vitamin C: two capsules twice daily
- organic selenium (selenium yeast): 400 mcg daily
- wild chaga mushroom extract (emulsified in a dropper bottle): 40 drops twice daily
- wild chaga mushroom expresso: one cup twice daily
- natural-source vitamin E, ideally from sunflower seed oil: two capsules daily
- natural-source B complex powder: three tablespoons daily
- wild raw greens extract as a source of riboflavin, as drops under the tongue: 20 drops twice daily
- wild raw berries extracts as drops under the tongue: 20 drops twice daily
- steam-extracted wild sockeye salmon oil rich in astaxanthin, vitamin A, and vitamin D (powerful Polar-source): teaspoonful daily
- juice of wild oregano: an ounce daily

Note: professional athletes may wish to double or triple these dosages. Also, competitive players may benefit from taking doses right before activities.

Inflammation: forest cures to the rescue

In traditional use forest medicines are used to fight both pain and inflammation. In particular, the barks of certain trees and also chaga mushroom have been used for this purpose. So have the tree buds and also their sap. Even the needles and leaves of certain trees have been used to fight pain and inflammation. With particular emphasis on chaga let us look at the studies, which confirm antiinflammatory powers of such natural medicines.

Inflammation is related to the immune system. Regarding arthritis there is also an immune connection. It is estimated that some 80% of arthritis cases are due to infection. Much of the infection originates in the gut as well as, possibly, the roots of the teeth and jaw bones. These regions of infestation are called foci of infection. Here, obviously, it is the infection which causes the inflammation. Additionally, cancer is an inflammatory condition, and chaga mushroom extract, as well as birch bark extract and poplar bud extract, are all effective anticancer agents. This proves that they are also highly antiinflammatory. The data supports this. In Korea a study was done to test just how chaga mushroom extract blocks inflammation. The investigators found that it effectively blocks the production of the enzymes which mediate the process. Both nitric oxide synthase and cyclooxygenase (COX-2) production were effectively inhibited, and these enzymes are among the most powerful mediators of inflammation in the body. This is why the researchers concluded that rather than a mere mushroom this mushroom is a medicine and that it, surely, will prove useful clinically in the treatment of inflammation.

In Poland it is well known that chaga fights pain syndromes. This, it is believed, is through the ability of its components to modulate the immune system. Uniquely, this mushroom has a direct, positive action on the key physiological warriors against inflammation, which are the white blood cells. Chaga induces the production of new, healthy white blood cells from the bone marrow and lymphocytes. This not only greatly increases the resistance to disease, but it also is essential for its eradication.

Clearly, the mushroom, noted the researchers, activated the immune cells. This was readily measurable, because through the ingestion of chaga there was an increase in key compounds produced by these cells such as interleukins, tumor necrosis factor, and gamma interferon. All such substances are powerful in reversing inflammation as well as the root of inflammation, which is infection.

C. Lull publishing in *Mediators of Inflammation* said that in certain conditions mushroom extracts such as chaga, rich in beta glucan, "have profound effects" in reversing inflammation, particularly in the fight against autoimmune diseases and chronic allergic conditions. She and her group concluded that mushroom extracts are effective against autoimmune and allergy-induced disease because of their capacity to activate an effective immune response against these conditions. Chaga mushroom is one of the most potent sources of beta glucan. Commercial supplements, which contain purified forms of this substance, are usually derived from baker's yeast. The latter may cause allergic reactions. Thus, for the ingestion of beta glucan chaga mushroom and other forest mushrooms, such as wild oyster mushroom, are the preferred sources. Regardless, through the ingestion of potent mushroom extracts containing beta glucan the activity of white blood cells is greatly enhanced. This is of importance in all diseases. Certainly, this is because these cells protect the body against infection. Yet, they have numerous other functions such as the reversal of allergic toxicity and also a kind of garbage control function, where the white blood cells actually surround and digest undesirable materials.

Some people might worry that chaga mushroom extract and/or beta glucan is an immune stimulant. These are the people who are often told by their doctors to avoid such substances. With chaga and similar forest mushrooms this is the opposite of the case, because rather than acting to stimulate the immune system or to over-stimulate it, they create balance. Notes Lull the components of medicinal mushrooms, particularly glucan, "make the immune system work better, without becoming overactive." They accomplish this, she says, by the most ideal mechanism, which is to make the body work more normally, notably the white blood cells. Chaga causes these cells to improve their ability to trap and destroy foreign invaders and also foreign substances, including allergens.

Korean investigators are well aware of the antiinflammatory actions of chaga mushroom. In the nutrition industry people know that, for instance, enzymes fight inflammation. They are aware of turmeric and ginger as antiinflammatory agents. But mushrooms? This is not well known. Yet, in particular, tree mushrooms dramatically improve immune function, and it is this system, which mediates inflammation. So, it makes sense that high grade mushrooms would be a required part of the battle to halt pain and inflammation.

Chaga is particularly well researched in this regard. Because it is effective in such a wide range of diseases— diabetes, cancer, heart disease, lung conditions, and gastrointestinal disorders—investigators sought to discover the mechanism whereby it could halt inflammation, since all such diseases are associated with it. It was Korean researchers who took the lead in this. Publishing in the *Journal of Medicinal Food* (2007) they found that, without doubt, chaga extract relieves pain. Here, they made clear, this mushroom contains components which block the mediators of inflammation such as prostaglandins. It also, they determined, eases swelling and irritation and does so in a way superior to medication. In further studies to uncover the mechanism the investigators found that chaga blocks the production of key enzymes, notably nitric oxide synthase and cyclooxygenase (COX-2)—the same mechanism touted for potent drugs. The extract even prevented an inflammation mediator, the so-called nuclear factor kappa beta, from binding to the genes. That binding is a key component of the inflammatory cascade. This means that chaga extract is equally potent as any antiinflammatory drug but without the side effects. In fact, it is even more potent than such drugs, as demonstrated by the following:

> Mr. A. is a physician who suffered from a sudden onset of pain in the mid-back. The pain was deep in the rib area. It was so severe he thought it was a kidney stone, but this was ruled out. Whenever he moved, he screeched in pain. Also, the pain was worse with very deep breaths.
>
> Knowing the antiinflammatory power of chaga, he made a large cup of the expresso. After drinking this he noticed a reduction in the pain, which he found astonishing. Convinced it was the chaga he drank an additional two cups, plus he took the drops under the tongue. The deep-seated pain was reduced 95%. Said Mr. A. this was a tremendous result for any substance to achieve. No drug could create such permanent relief. The side effect, he reported to me, was that he noticed more energy and when taking these large doses of chaga, was able to wake up earlier in the morning.

Gastrointestinal effects

Mushroom tea made from tree fungi, such as chaga, has a long use in the Orient for disorders of the gut. The once-powerful Ainu people of northern Japan consumed tree mushrooms in hot water for stomach pain and inflammation. They also smoked the pulverized mushroom in a pipe ceremonially. They used to call this "eating the smoke," which obviously benefited them in some unknown way. A photograph of these people, as found in *Asian Biomedicine*, December, 2008, shows that these people were of strong stock. They stood upright, were well-built, and beautiful in appearance. Much of their dramatic features were apparently due to their regular consumption of tree mushrooms.

Obviously, these dramatic-appearing people had no major digestive disorders, as they were people of the most powerful stock known.

When taken in hot water or as emulsified drops under the tongue, chaga stimulates the production of bile. The bile is essential for the digestion of fat. Additionally, this substance is the body's natural soap, particularly for use in cleansing the intestinal walls. Without this soap food residues accumulate in the colon wall, leading to symptoms and, ultimately, disease.

Additionally, this mushroom, especially when combined with wild birch bark extract, is a potent germicide. It is largely germs which cause digestive disease. The emulsified chaga extract purges such germs, especially the various pathogenic bacteria and viruses, which are harbored within the gut wall.

Sterols are highly critical for the function of the digestive organs. These substances act to strengthen the cell membranes of the intestinal cells. These cells regenerate more rapidly than any others in the body. Essentially, the entire realm of the gastrointestinal cells, trillions of them, are regenerated every seven days. To rebuild each of these cells need a supply of sterols and, more specifically, steroids. Additionally, the digestive juice bile is made largely from steroids. Thus, these substances are equally important nutritionally as are amino acids, sugars, and vitamins.

A lack of steroids/sterols leads to degenerative disease, including degeneration of the intestinal and stomach walls. Thus, these substances are essential nutrients.

Gastritis, H. pylori, and ulcers

Traditionally, stomach disorders are a primary use for chaga mushroom. In Siberia it is well established as a cure for virtually all stomach conditions, especially gastritis and ulcers. Yet, this, too, means the mushroom is active against the bacteria H. pylori, since this is the primary cause of these disorders.

No one knows for sure why, traditionally, chaga has been so effective for stomach disorders, especially ulcers. It is presumed that this relates to its action against H. pylori. Regardless, since chaga is able to induce a state of normal immunity this alone would account for the improvement. The germ-fighting organs of the human body often become overwhelmed. Ultimately, they are virtually incapable of warding of disease-causing pathogens. They are also unable to cause the reversal of disease. Chaga stimulates local immunity. It causes the white blood cells to send messages to all the body calling for the purging of the invader(s). This includes the stomach invader H. pylori.

For the digestive tract the fact that chaga mushroom is rich in sterols proves invaluable, as these compounds are needed for the cell membranes, including the membranes of stomach cells. Because of inflammation, stress, infection, and other stressors the sterols can be damaged and/or depleted. This may lead to a sufficient breakdown in tissue, which allows infection and, therefore, ulceration to form. Additionally, in H. pylori and gastric ulcer there is low oxygen in the stomach wall. The levels of protective enzymes are also low. Chaga, with its rich content of oxygenated sterols and the highly oxygenated enzyme superoxide dismutase, corrects this. Of note green cabbage is high in this enzyme. Perhaps this explains how both these substances reverse gastric ulcers.

Treatment protocol

For stomach ulcer take emulsified wild chaga as drops under the tongue, 40 drops three times daily. Use also the expresso every morning and in extreme cases with every meal. Additionally, to cause direct destruction to H. pylori take the edible oil of wild oregano, true type, Mediterranean wild hand-picked, five or more drops under the tongue three times daily. Plus, take the emulsified poplar bud extract as drops under the tongue, 40 drops twice daily. Follow the same protocol for gastritis, but reduce the dosage by half. For duodenal ulcer follow the same protocol, with the addition of a high grade enzyme supplement, ideally with wild spices, including cardamom and coriander. As well coriander has a calming action on the small intestine. In particular, the juice of coriander is invaluable, about an ounce twice daily. In the event of stomach cancer follow the same protocol of H. plyori with the following additions and modifications:

- juice of wild oregano (12-ounce bottle): two ounces twice daily
- juice of wild rosemary (12-ounce bottle): at a different time than the oregano juice take two ounces twice daily
- drink a cup of the chaga expresso with each meal
- increase the dosage of emulsified chaga drops, 50 drops four times daily
- eat wild raw honey, as needed
- eat yogurt instead of fermented cheese or milk; this should be consumed on an empty stomach with added extra virgin olive oil, sea salt, and crude whole wild oregano herb
- juice of organic cabbage, eight or more ounces daily

Cardiovascular effects

It is well established that mushrooms are food for the heart. In fact, it has been determined, regular mushroom users are less vulnerable to heart disease than non-users. This was thought to be due to the rich content in mushrooms of minerals, notably the heart friendly selenium and manganese. Yet, there are other components in wild mushrooms which account for this protective effect. This was determined by Japanese investigators, who publishing in *Life Sciences* determined a refined action of forest mushrooms (chaga) on the heart. It was determined that bioglycans isolated from the mushroom in a tiny concentration (about 1/10,000 of a percent) enhanced the pumping power of the heart. This was observed as a reduction in the time required for the firing of impulses in the nerve center of the heart, known as the venous sinus. Thus, the heart after treatment with the chaga compound pumped more vigorously. The mechanism of the mushroom extract was determined, which is that it acted as a natural and non-toxic calcium channel blocker.

Another effect of chaga relates to blood coagulation. The mushroom extract has a direct effect on platelet function, preventing excessive aggregation. In fact, this is of value both in heart disease and cancer as well as diabetes. All such diseases are associated with an increased thickness of the blood due to hyperactive platelets. A solvent extract of chaga proved to be the most potent, having an 80%-plus inhibitory activity. This is a vast power, which would prove invaluable in the treatment of chronic circulatory diseases as well as cancer. Investigators immediately realized the value in cancer treatment, since this disease is associated with thick blood. Thus, they furthered their studies by testing mice vulnerable to cancer. In these mice the chaga extract also showed a high capacity to prevent congealed blood. Cancer spreads in the environment of thick blood with hyperactive platelets, while its growth and spread is blocked in an environment of normally functioning platelets and thin blood.

The sterols and steroids in chaga are also essential components for cardiovascular health. This is because these substances act as structural components for the integrity of the heart muscle as well as the arteries. The sterols/steroids help essentially tighten up the membranes. In this regard their functions are invaluable. A strong heart means a long life, a fact which is indisputable. The fact that chaga extract revives both the cardiovascular system and immune system is significant. This means that this sophisticated complex is a true health food necessary for the regeneration of the body and, therefore, the maintenance of ideal health.

The value of the sterols in chaga and wild birch bark for heart and arterial disease must be emphasized. These waxes are contrary to popular belief essential for the health of the cardiovascular system. The infrastructure of the heart muscle cells are built with cholesterol molecules. The same is true of the structure of the arteries. With birch bark and chaga these are essentially raw types of cholesterol, rather, these molecules are wild. Plus, since this type of 'cholesterol' is from trees these are tough molecules.

This toughness is invaluable for the heart and arteries, which are under constant pressure for mere survival. Here is how chaga/birch bark help assist this. For instance, the wild-source sterols are incorporated into the cell walls of the heart muscle. Here, in what is the opposite of what most people understand these cholesterol-like molecules make the heart muscle fibers flexible. This flexibility improves the pumping power of the heart and also protects it from injury. The same is true of the arteries. Flexible arteries have a long life, while brittle ones readily degenerate. The same is true of the heart, because as long as the muscle fibers of this tissue remain pliable the heart can essentially pump forever. In this manner chaga and birch bark extend lifespan.

The heart and arteries absorb these mushroom sterols and make major use of them. This is a major reason which explains the power of these foods to extend lifespan. Yes, truly chaga and birch bark are not merely natural medicines for the cardiovascular system, but, rather, they are its food. For the maintenance of powerful heart and arteries chaga as a hot water drink (expresso) and oregano oil-emulsified drops, should be taken on a regular basis. Even a mere 20 drops daily of the emulsified extract is significant protection.

For people with heart disease chaga is part of the answer. Birch bark is another key; both chaga and birch bark are rich in the types of sterols which strengthen the heart muscle. These molecules are among the most essential of all substances for heart health. Sterols not only strengthen heart muscle tissue but also make it more flexible. This will increase its resistance to wear and tear. Also, sterols help prevent the heart valves from degenerating. They also act as a fuel source for the heart muscle. Thus, the regular intake of emulsions of chaga mushroom and/or white birch bark are exceedingly protective for this organ.

The wild raw forest greens extract and, particularly, the wild raw berries extract are also a critical part of the protocol. Poplar bud is also essential, since it is a natural blood thinner and also helps halt oxidative damage to the heart and arterial walls. Emulsified extract of poplar bud has a high ORAC level. Thus, the regular intake of such an extract would provide a vast degree of protection for both the arteries and the heart against oxidative damage. In addition, vitamin D is essential for cardiovascular health, as are the B vitamins. Deficiencies of these nutrients greatly weaken the heart. The following is a treatment protocol for heart and circulatory conditions, including cardiac arrhythmia, hardening of the arteries, mitral valve prolapse, coronary artery disease, congestive heart failure, and stroke:

- oil of wild oregano (as a means for clearing fungi and bacteria from the blood and also increasing the pumping power of this organ): three to five drops under the tongue once or twice daily

- wild chaga drops, emulsified in extra virgin olive oil and raw vinegar: 20 or more drops under the tongue twice daily
- raw wild poplar bud extract as drops under the tongue, 40 or more drops twice daily
- purely natural B complex concentrate made from a combination of torula yeast, royal jelly, and rice brown/germ
- vitamin A and D from a crude whole food source (wild Polar-source sockeye salmon oil is the superior source for these)

The respiratory system: powerful effects

It is well established that both chaga mushroom and birch bark extract are potent medicines for the respiratory system. Disorders of this system are one of the primary historical uses for these medicines.

Both these natural medicines are antifungal agents. They also boost the immune response against viruses and bacteria as well as fungi. The majority of respiratory conditions are due to infections, with fungi playing the most predominant role. The fungi lodge in the respiratory tissues chronically, and the immune system is unable to eradicate them. Thus, it needs a boost, and this boost comes from tree medicines, particularly emulsified wild chaga.

A great deal of respiratory disease is caused by tuberculosis. A second major category is chronic fungus, which is the key cause of chronic sinus disorders, earaches, and bronchitis. Fungal infection also plays a role in asthma. Chaga and birch bark emulsions are both active against the tubercular germs and various fungi, as is demonstrated by the following case history:

Ms. K., a 49-year-old office worker, had a major dilemma, which was a chronic earache. A problem of over a year in duration she attempted a number of remedies to cure it, including oil of wild oregano. However, the infection persisted. Her son, a worker for a nutritional supplement company, brought home a bottle of emulsified wild chaga mushroom extract. In desperation she tried this, taking 40 drops sublingually, and noticed an immediate improvement. Within a day, she reported, the chronic earache was eliminated.

In chronic respiratory infections the capacity of the immune system is low. Thus, infections readily become established. The use of antibiotics worsens this by causing deep-seated fungal infestation. This demonstrates the need for natural medicines which bolster immune function. This is precisely what is achieved by sterol-rich tree medicines. In particular, emulsified chaga directly activates white blood cells through the action of beta glucan. This substance increases the capacity of lymphocytes to clear noxious viruses and fungi as well as the ubiquitous tubercular germ. With chaga there is also the rich content of SOD, the latter being needed for the processing of oxygen in the lungs and also for the prevention of oxygen-induced lung cell damage. Respiratory conditions which are positively affected by chaga and birch bark extracts include sinusitis, otitis media, serous otitis media, laryngitis, bronchitis, pneumonia, histoplasmosis, coccidiomycosis, blastomycosis, aspergillosis, and tuberculosis.

In any respiratory condition chaga must be used. This is true both of acute and chronic conditions. The chaga emulsion boosts the immune system's ability to clear pathogens from the lungs. This is an invaluable function, since severe respiratory infections can lead to chronic disease and even fatality. Yet, with a powerful immune system such toxicity is effectively resisted. It is chaga mushroom emulsion, as well as the wild chaga expresso, which imparts such immune power.

Dermatological effects

Chaga and birch bark have potent actions on the health of the skin. In particular, the actions of chaga against skin diseases have been well studied. The effects are highly significant, as demonstrated by the fact that in Asia, eastern Europe, and Russia skin creams containing chaga are a mainstay for the treatment of skin disorders as well as for the prevention of aging.

Regarding skin diseases it has been determined that many of the chronic types, such as eczema, rosacea, and psoriasis, are due to disorders of the immune system. These disorders lead to a breakdown in tissue integrity and therefore infection. The infection is often caused by common skin bacteria and fungi, including the yeast *Pitysporum ovale* and the bacteria *Staphylococcus epidermidis* and *Propionibacterium acnes*. In one investigation it was found that extract of medicinal mushroom inhibited the growth of all three of these germs, which may explain the folk use of tree mushrooms against psoriasis, eczema, and acne. It has also been determined that the sterols in medicinal mushrooms have a modest inhibitory action against the fungi which cause athlete's foot and toenail fungus. As noted in *The Pharmalogical Potential of Mushrooms* in South Africa medicinal mushrooms are used to treat sunburn, and in Yemen diaper rash. In addition to their antifungal properties the sterols of medicinal mushrooms, particularly those found in chaga, are highly soothing when applied to skin. Plus, the rich content of SOD may account for the fact that extracts of this mushroom have been demonstrated to ease and even reverse skin disorders.

Regarding rosacea this has been associated with inflammation and infection of the stomach lining. No doubt, in many cases there is associated H. plyori infection. Chaga is a well known cure for stomach disorders. In this manner it is active against rosacea, although it is also effective, when applied topically. Regardless, chaga is a worthy natural medicine for any skin disorder, particularly those associated with inflammatory lesions. Here, it has the dual function of potency, whether taken internally or applied topically. There is also the benefit of sublingual administration, that is through the intake of the emulsified chaga drops, which are ideal for skin afflictions of the head and neck.

Aging of the skin, as well as various precancerous skin lesions, respond to chaga therapy. Thus, it should be consumed as a preferred treatment for excessive wrinkling, thinning of the skin, brown/liver spots, senile keratoses, and skin tags. Here, again it can be applied topically as well as taken internally.

Musculoskeletal effects

The musculoskeletal system is tied to the immune system. It is the immune system which largely mediates inflammation, and this includes any inflammatory processes which occur in the muscles, bones, and joints. Additionally, the gut is connected to the health of this system. Thus, disorders of the gut readily lead to symptoms and/or diseases of the joints and muscles.

There is another power in the tree medicines that may account for their power in musculoskeletal health. This is their content of actual anti-pain and antiinflammatory agents. Such agents include salicin, benzoin, benzoic acid, cinnaminic acid, caffeic acid, betulin, lanosterin, and betulinic acid.

Furthermore, tree medicines are the source of a wide range of sterols. These sterols are hormone-like. The steroids (and sterols) are highly antiinflammatory. These are found in rich amounts in the barks and buds of trees as well as in tree fungi, particularly chaga and oyster mushrooms.

Additionally, all tree medicines bolster adrenal function. It is these glands which are involved in the entire stress response. The adrenal glands also help modulate inflammation. Deficiency of adrenal steroids (hormones) readily leads to inflammatory disorders and chronic pain.

It is the bark of trees, that of the white willow, which provided aspirin, the world's first pain-killing drug. Thus, in particular for pain syndromes and diseases of inflammation tree bark medicines, such as the emulsified wild chaga drops and the birch-bark fortified chaga expresso, offer significant powers. Yet, the most potent source of natural pain killing substances are the buds of certain trees, notably birch and especially poplar buds.

So, there are a number of mechanisms whereby medicines from northern forests can aid disorders of the muscles, bones, and joints. These medicines replace the typical drugs, because they contain the same essential compounds and have a similar mechanism of action—without the side effects. To a large degree they are more effective than the drugs—aspirin, acetaminophen, opiates, and COX-2 inhibitors—because they offer varied mechanisms of actions. For instance, in addition to the chaga poplar bud extract boosts adrenal function.

Vitamin C is also needed for the health of the musculoskeletal system, as are B vitamins, vitamin A, vitamin D, and minerals. Natural-source nutrients are more powerful biologically than the synthetic, that is the type typically found in multiple vitamin tablets.

There is another major issue regarding chaga's influence on structural disorders, an influence also exerted by birch bark concentrates. This relates to tuberculosis of the bones. Globally, there are millions of people who suffer from this. It is an insidious disease. It may be manifested by nothing more than a chronic sense of heaviness or stiffness in the low back, mid-back, and neck. The neck may be torqued;

there may be swollen glands chronically in this region. There may also be distortion of the upper spinal column with a swelling in the thoracic spine, a condition known as Pott's disease.

For TB of the bone chaga is the most infamous cure. Siberian tribesmen, somewhat vulnerable to this disease due to their climate and diet, have proved repeatedly its powers. This natural medicine dramatically increases the immune powers of the body against the exceedingly stubborn tubercular germ. It is one of the few natural medicines with the powers to reverse TB infection/damage to the bones, as demonstrated by the following case history:

> Mr. A., a 55-year old man of Mediterranean descent, suffered from chronic stiffness of the neck with a knot sensation on the left side. He had been exposed to TB numerous times and had apparently developed a chronic case. In addition to the neck stiffness he developed chronic stiffness in the upper back with a Pott's disease-like swelling in the middle of the spine. Chaga therapy, as the emulsified spice oil-based drops, was begun, along with drops of emulsified birch bark. Within a few minutes of taking the chaga he noticed a major improvement in the knot in the neck: some 80% relief. Gradually, the stiffness in all regions improved, and there was a visible benefit. The Pott's disease-like swelling in the upper back was reduced by 70%.

Now, with tree medicines there is hope for chronic pain as well as diseases associated with inflammation. Here, nature is more powerful than drugs. Even natural aspirin, such as salicin, the type found in poplar buds, is more effective than the synthetic form. Plus, unlike synthetic aspirin there is no possibility of fatality from the intake of poplar buds or their extracts. Furthermore, with the natural extract there are numerous secondary effects such as improvement in skin tone, improved digestion, enhanced immunity, and halting of the aging process.

Treatment of pain/inflammation syndromes must incorporate all of the aforementioned, as follows:

Treatment protocol

For any condition manifested by pain and/or inflammation take:

- emulsified wild chaga drops: 20 or more drops under the tongue three times daily
- wild chaga expresso, one or more cups daily
- crude whole food vitamin C capsules consisting of wild raw camu camu plus acerola and rose hips: two capsules twice daily
- crude wild emulsified poplar bud extract (in extra virgin olive oil and raw apple cider vinegar): 40 drops twice daily
- optional: crude unfiltered whole food sockeye salmon oil from the wild fish (Polar-source): two teaspoons daily or 10 gelcaps daily

Metabolic/endocrine effects

The effects of forest medicines, particularly the highly unique and chemically diverse chaga mushroom, is profound. These various forest cures have a vast array of natural compounds which act upon metabolism. These are the sterols which are, essentially the hormones and pre-hormones. These large plans also contain a variety of enzymes which they contain that directly influence the metabolic process. Regardless, any substance(s) powerful enough to keep alive massive trees will surely have a major impact upon the human body.

Any substance which alters metabolism is a hormone. Thus, it is no surprise that hormone-rich chaga mushroom does this. So, it is hormone-like. Birch bark extract also does this, so it, too, is a kind of hormonal agent. Additionally, the buds of trees are essentially concentrates of hormones, so, for instance, poplar bud extract supports the hormonal system.

Chaga has a massive action against free-radicals. By definition free radicals are toxic forms of oxygen, which are produced as a result of normal or noxious metabolic processes. These forms of oxygen readily damage cells.

It makes sense that tree medicines are the answer for free radical damage. Trees produce their own substances which quench free radicals. Substances in the white birch bark have a potent action on the metabolism of oxygen in the body. In fact, these substances cause any oxygen which is being burned in the body to be used more efficiently. This is true most greatly of tree extracts from far northern forests, which is the source of both the emulsion and the expresso. Only trees in cold climates are used, the chaga itself being harvested from entirely remote northern regions.

Chaga and birch bark extract are so potent that they even reverse poor oxygen metabolism. Even if a person is hypoxic, meaning they lack sufficient oxygen in the body, the forest medicines prove effective. Oxygen is the energy-force for all reactions in human cells. People with certain diseases, notably Alzheimer's disease, Parkinson's disease, ALS, multiple sclerosis, heart disease, psoriasis, diabetes, and cancer, are unable to efficiently use this force.

There may be physical signs of low oxygen. These signs include enlargement of the surface blood vessels of the face, usually about the cheeks and nose as well as on the cornea of the eyes. The typical blood-shot eye appearance is a sign of low oxygen. It is also a sign of riboflavin deficiency. Chaga contains this nutrient as do wild, raw forest greens. Another sign of the deficiency is notable in the fingernails, where there is a lack of moons. Normally, there should be obvious moons, which are semicircles of a lighter color at the base of the nail bed. When this is lacking on the first, second, and third finger, then, a defect in oxygen metabolism is confirmed.

This low oxygen is corrected through the intake of chaga, because this mushroom causes the cells of the human body to adapt to a lack of oxygen. Plus, whatever oxygen is available as a result of chaga/birch bark the cells use it more efficiently. This is in part the result of their rich enzyme content, especially SOD, which is the key enzyme for controlling oxygen metabolism. Plus, this mushroom is a top source of molecular oxygen in the form of polyphenols and sterols. In this regard sublingual drops are ideal, since these substances are difficult to absorb from the gut.

For most humans metabolism is too slow. For a few it is too fast. Regardless, in all cases the utilization of oxygen is impaired. All people could use more of this molecule or make better use of the oxygen they have. Any increase in this life-giving gas makes a positive impact on health. Just think about it, how healthy and invigorated a person feels when having a few breaths of fresh air, say, for instance, in a forested area? There is no doubt about the impact. Chaga is like bringing the forest to the individual, because it contains rich supplies of molecular oxygen, which it traps from the forest air.

The main tree medicines mentioned in this book, the chaga expresso, emulsified chaga extract, and the poplar bud extract, are all derived from far northern trees. Thus, they are rich in trapped molecular oxygen. When this molecular oxygen is consumed, it is released in the body to bolster metabolic processes. There could be no greater power than this for human health and for the cure of human disease.

In this regard the function of the thyroid must be considered. People with low function—hypothyroidism—

have poor oxygen utilization. Their oxygen metabolism can be 1/10 or less of normal. This leads to a wide range of physical disorders and symptoms. Diseases caused by the low oxygen metabolism of hypothyroidism include heart disease, high blood pressure, diabetes, vasculitis, congestive heart failure, atrial fibrillation, arthritis, and cancer. For more information about the signs and symptoms of low thyroid function, as well as the physical features, see the book *The Body Shape Diet* (Knowledge House Publishers, same author).

Chaga and birch bark are highly oxygenated. The sterols alone are a rich source of biologically active oxygen, and with chaga the content of the oxygen-bearing enzyme SOD is supreme. This is why the intake of these extracts is particularly effective in this condition. Additionally, in low thyroid function fungal infection is often rampant. Here again chaga and birch bark come to the rescue by assisting the immune system in purging fungal infestation.

The adrenal glands also benefit from these extracts in particular the chaga. The rich sterol content of chaga and birch bark help calm these glands. This is because the sterols provide the biological molecules needed for the synthesis of adrenal hormones. Additionally, the SOD content of this mushroom is invaluable, since this enzyme is needed for the production of key adrenal steroids such as aldosterone, cortisol, DHEA, and androgens.

In particular, the adrenal glands are highly vulnerable to stress. Today, people live in a high stress world. There is always a need for substances which support the function of these glands. Chaga mushroom emulsion is one of the most powerful substances for supporting adrenal function known. In anyone with weak adrenals this must be taken routinely and in some cases as a daily supplement. This is merely for the maintenance of good health and a normal life.

Chaga's ultimate power—the supreme potency of chromogenic complex

The supreme power in chaga relates to its content of a highly rare substance, superoxide dismutase (SOD). On a weight basis, the chaga mushroom is richer in SOD than any other known substance. Incredibly, from 30% to 40% of the entire weight of the mushroom is SOD in a unique form known as chromogenic complex. A chromogenic substance is an indication of high energy activity. It defines substances which interact with light to trap its energy. In SOD this is done via its content of protein-bound minerals, notably zinc, copper, and manganese. The interaction of the light with the minerals leads to a pigment—a chromogen.

The SOD value per gram in chaga is some 35 times higher than that found in other well known medicinal mushrooms such as lingzhi, and agaricus. This explains the dark blackish-brown color of chaga, which is proof of trapped biological energy from the sun. This is also why the ingestion of this mushroom creates such vast power in the body. It is a power unmatched by any other substance.

Regardless, it has always been known that enzymes are one of the key medicinal substances in mushrooms. Moreover, SOD is such a substance. However, rather than the typical enzyme, which is digestive, this is an antioxidant enzyme, which is of profound importance. Naturally produced in the body, SOD is the primary antioxidant enzyme associated with a long, healthy life. This powerful enzyme complex is produced and strategically placed within all cells of the body. However, as mentioned previously levels of this enzyme decline dramatically with age. This is why declining SOD levels is the key marker for premature aging. Thus, it should be obvious that keeping tissue levels of this molecule as high as possible is essential for ideal health as well as a long and vigorous life.

There are few food sources of SOD, and mushrooms are one of the best. Yet, of all mushrooms only chaga contains this substance in dense amounts. Chaga produces this molecule aggressively while feeding on living birch trees. The birch tree itself is an effective system for trapping oxygen, thus, this is why chaga thrives on it. Without a steady source of biological oxygen, the chaga cannot survive. The mushroom incorporates the birch tree's oxygen when synthesizing the SOD. The "O" in this term stands for molecular oxygen.

Oxygen is essential to life. It is more essential than food or water. A person can live for weeks without food and up to two weeks without water. However, without air an average person will not last much longer than a couple minutes. So, to be in optimal health it is necessary to consume oxygen in as many forms as possible, including food and beverage. In this regard SOD is one of the most potent food forms of oxygen known.

Vaccination and the destruction of health: forest cures to the rescue

Vaccinated people are in major need of tree medicines. Anyone who has been heavily vaccinated has been compromised. There is no health benefit to these injections, only harm. Thus, the toxic components must be purged from the body.

Vaccines introduce a wide range of animal pathogens and even some human ones. These drugs are extensively contaminated with disease-causing microbes. It was the world's top vaccine researcher, Maurice Helliman, who confirmed this, saying that the standard medical vaccines are nothing more than "bargain basement" drugs. This means they are produced merely for financial gain in the most crude way conceivable.

Helliman said the vaccines are usually contaminated. So noted the British physician W. D. Clark, who established the scope of the contamination over a century ago. Noted Clark the massive increase in cancer incidence in modern society is due virtually exclusively to these vile agents.

Vaccines introduce live viruses, bacteria, molds, and fungi. They force into the body various mutated germs, which are poorly recognized by the immune system. According to vaccine insider John Rapport these drugs even introduce parasites, for instance, amebas. Additionally, vaccines contain noxious chemicals as well as heavy metals, including mercury, aluminum, formaldehyde, aspartame, sulfites, and MSG. Millions of people are allergic and/or sensitive to such substances.

No wonder that a wide range of diseases are directly associated with vaccination. People have no idea how dangerous are these poisonous needles. Nor do they routinely associate any symptoms or diseases with their administration. Vaccines don't merely cause symptoms or diseases in the immediate aftermath of the injections but, rather, usually cause these months, years, or even decades later.

Through intimidation they are forced upon the children. It is as if there are powerful people who want the people sickened or at least weakened. There is no doubt about it those who reject the vaccines and merely take care of their health are far more powerful in vitality than the heavily vaccinated.

Regardless, forest cures are one of those few natural therapies capable of causing the needed regeneration of cell membranes. Healthy cell membranes means, essentially, freedom from disease. It is also the method to achieve the greatest degree of recovery from inoculations. Clearly, there are hundreds of syndromes and diseases caused by vaccinations. Moreover, there is little if any hope for the reversal of these diseases unless the noxious vaccine components are purged. A list of diseases/syndromes caused by vaccination includes:

- Crohn's disease
- ulcerative colitis
- ankylosing spondylitis
- systemic lupus
- juvenile rheumatoid arthritis
- diabetes type 1
- Alzheimer's disease
- Parkinson's disease
- multiple sclerosis
- ALS (Lou Gehrig's disease)
- Gullaine-Barré syndrome
- Bell's palsy
- myasthenia gravis
- pericarditis
- fibromyalgia
- chronic fatigue syndrome
- psoriasis and/or eczema
- pemphigus
- rheumatoid arthritis
- chronic viral syndrome
- tuberculosis

In addition, the following cancers are largely induced by the highly destructive microbes found in vaccinations:

- lymphoma
- leukemia
- brain cancer (excluding those cancers caused by cell phones and other forms of radiation)
- lung cancer, particularly mesothelioma
- sarcoma
- breast cancer (primarily the inflammatory type)
- colon cancer

This proves that there is much need to reverse vaccine-induced pathology. Yet, what are people to do? They have already been extensively poisoned. It would only make it worse to take substances which further burden the tissues. Enter the power of forest cures. These cures never burden the body nor cause any side-effects. Rather, they create the opposite result, which is monumental relief from symptoms. They also act to actually reverse disease.

In particular, chaga and birch bark extracts are invaluable for reversing any damage. This is because the sterols in these forest medicines bolster immune function, rather, normalize it. This is what is required to purge the vaccine pathogens from the body. Furthermore, the greater the pathogen level the more aggressive must be the chaga therapy. Additionally, the sterols are preventive. This is because they aid in the rebuilding of cell membranes. This greatly enhances the resistance of the cells against the pathogens introduced into the body through vaccination. It is these pathogens that are largely responsible for the diseases that result from these poisonous needles. To recover from the damage it is crucial to rebuild the cell membranes, particularly those of the brain, spinal cord, and peripheral nerves. The most potent medicines for achieving this are the wild, raw chaga mushroom emulsion, the wild chaga/birch bark expresso, and the wild, raw birch bark emulsion.

In fact, the regeneration of the cell membranes is one of the most critical secrets to great health. This is greatly achieved by wild chaga mushroom extract, particularly the spice oil emulsion. Here, the maximum degree of absorption of these crucial substances is achieved so they can be utilized by the cells throughout the body. Through the wild, raw chaga extract emulsion as well as the birch bark-enhanced wild chaga expresso, vaccine injury may be reversed. Other supplements, however, may be of value in inducing this regeneration, including germ-killing spice oils and key vitamins for strengthening the immune system. In addition, essential fatty acids and fatty fish oils are critical for nourishing and rebuilding cells. The following is a thorough protocol for causing the return of health in the event of vaccine injury:

- wild, raw emulsified chaga extract (as drops under the tongue): 20 or more drops twice daily
- wild, raw chaga-birch bark expresso: drink a cup once daily
- oil of wild oregano, Mediterranean hand-picked: 5 to 10 drops twice daily
- healthy bacterial supplement, that is Ecologic 500: as directed (take a few hours after taking the oregano oil)
- crude whole food natural vitamin A and D source, ideally wild sockeye salmon oil or cod liver oil: two teaspoons daily or every other day
- crude whole food vitamin C, ideally as a combination of wild camu camu and acerola: two capsules twice daily
- whole food Amazon-source sacha inchi oil: one teaspoon daily

In addition, for some people a purge is necessary. This is achieved through the use of wild whole greens, which are hand-picked from the remote forests. The extracts are preserved raw and then emulsified in organic extra virgin olive oil, organic black seed oil, and organic apple cider vinegar. This is taken as a purging agent to cleanse (decontaminate) the liver, gallbladder, spleen, and blood. It has no harshness and no laxative effect. Thus, it may be freely taken for decontamination purposes. For extreme cases of vaccine intoxication it is ideal to take such a purge for at least one month and preferably two months. This ideal dose is one to two ounces daily, and this can be taken daily until all function is normalized. At a minimum this should be taken for a month.

Chapter Eight

The Power of Sterols

Without sterols or, rather, steroids there would be no life. These substances are essential for a whole range of functions. They are the key essential raw materials for making life-giving hormones.They are also essential for fat digestion as well as cell membrane health. In the event of a total dietary deficiency, or deficiency in internal production, because the body makes steroid molecules daily in vast amounts, there would be systematic degeneration. Disease would strike, particularly sudden infection, heart disease, arthritis, and cancer. Ultimately, there would be premature death. Thus, for human health steroids or sterols are equally important as vitamins, minerals, and protein.

The sterols and saponins: key chaga ingredients

There is no doubt that chaga is a highly unusual food. While it is not a true plant or animal it has features of both. One of these features is the content of substances similar to animal steroids. These substances are known as sterols and saponins.

In antiquity mushrooms were regarded much differently than they are today. They were held in the highest status possible. This was largely due to their medicinal properties. The ancients discovered that rather than a mere accent to food certain mushrooms are potent medicines. For centuries the Chinese, Japanese, Koreans, and Siberians treasured them as divine gifts. As mentioned previously the Greeks held them as giving super-human strength. This is largely the result of the rich content in mushrooms of the cholesterol- and hormone-like sterols, which, when ingested, create great physical prowess.

The sterol content of chaga is highly significant. Moreover, these sterols are exceedingly medicinal. They are, for instance, of great benefit to the body nutritionally. It is also important to realize that these molecules are highly electrically charged and are also rich in molecular oxygen. Thus, they exert a significant influence upon metabolism, including the metabolic function of the central nervous system.

One reason chaga must make sterols is related to weather. Sterols are a kind of insulation. Chaga, as well as birch trees, thrives at temperatures as low as -70 degrees Centigrade. Regarding both these plants it is their inordinately rich content of sterols that gives them the strength to survive such harshness.

Most of the definitive studies on chaga and its sterol content have been performed by Dr. Kristi Kahlos at the University of Helsinki's School of Pharmacy. Here, she and her colleagues found that chaga contains a variety of sterols of great biological activity. It must be realized that the human body makes massive use of its sterols or, rather, steroids, primarily in the production of key substances, known as hormones. Yet, as mentioned previously the body also uses these compounds for structural integrity. The sterols of chaga, for instance, are readily incorporated into the walls of human cells. Here, they are used to strengthen existing cells and also aid in the production of new ones. Even the creation of the insulation of brain and nerve tissue, the myelin sheath, is steroid-dependent. Thus, for any disease associated with a breakdown of the myelin sheath, such as multiple sclerosis, ALS, and autism, chaga mushroom is essential. Yet, there is a caveat. The sterols from plant sources as a rule are difficult to absorb. Emulsification vastly aids in the absorption of these critical sterols, particularly if the emulsion is consumed as sublingual drops.

Sterols and the immune system

Kahlos found significant anti-tumor activity of the chaga extract, which may largely be the result of its sterol content. She also discovered that this mushroom is antiviral, with specific activity against flu viruses. These anti-viral and anti-tumor sterols are also found in significant amounts in birch bark, demonstrating the importance of a combination of these two natural medicines. In a dry, raw state both birch bark and chaga lend themselves to a hot water infusion, where the hot water acts to extract the sterols. The longer this is allowed to set after adding the hot water the greater will be the degree of steroid extraction (a maximum of three days at room temperature).

The combined approach has been emphasized through the results of scientific studies. It was again G. M. Fedosseva of Irkutsk State Medical University who made it clear that for maximum power the two must be combined. The medicinal powers of chaga are enhanced, she notes, by adding the birch bark, since this bark contains high amounts of sterols known to strengthen the immune response and even to exert direct action against diseased cells such as cancerous cells. These sterols are betulin, lupeol, inotodiol, and betulinic acid. Then, this makes a chaga/birch bark natural medicine a sterol powerhouse—and sterols and their derivatives, the steroids, are largely the basis of life. They are also the basis of the prevention of noxious diseases. Notes Fedosseva these birch bark sterols are so powerful that they decimate cancer by causing programmed cell death known as apoptosis. Of all medicinal mushrooms chaga contains the greatest density of medicinal sterols. To gain such synergistic power look for a chaga mushroom-based drink which also contains birch bark and maca. This provides a triple synergy of sterol power, all from the most natural and wild sources possible. This is because cold weather creates sufficient stress on the plants to cause the production of such sterols, and all these are from cold weather plants.

There is a uniqueness regarding chaga that must be described. Surely, there are numerous medicinal mushrooms. Plus, these growths contain a dense amount of nutrients, which is of value in human nutrition. For these reasons wild or organic mushrooms should be consumed, that is for those who are not sensitive to fungi. However, regarding medicinal mushrooms for reversing disease in many respects chaga alone is sufficient. It may be sufficient in most people to take only chaga for the desired effects. This is because this unique mushroom vastly supercedes all others in therapeutic power. Russian and Japanese investigators claim that chaga is some 100 times more powerful than its closest competitors such as maitake. Thus, for those who take this mushroom the intake of extracts of, for instance, maitake and reishi, may well be redundant.

An exception appears to be the oyster mushroom. This has a number of novel properties, and, thus, in some categories it is nearly equal to chaga. The most ideal type of oyster mushroom is the far northern type. Yet, if a person could pick one mushroom, surely, it would be chaga. Thus, to gain the benefits of those sterols the intake of the emulsion, as drops under the tongue, are required.

Lack of sterols: key cause of disease

Westin Price, D.D.S., proved decades ago that steroidal compounds play a key role in human health. That role was regarded of such critical importance that these substances were deemed the secret to vigorous health and were, therefore, deemed "factor X." Then, no one was sure what constituted these factors, but it was known that they were found primarily in animal foods and to a lesser degree in highly fatty vegetable foods (or oils). Plants are relatively weak in this factor. However, mushrooms, being a kind of in-between organism, contain considerable amounts. So do yeasts such as brewer's, baker's, and torula.

Chaga has many of these X-factor substances in a precursor form, that is as sterols. However, unaltered, these sterols are poorly absorbed, and, thus, for a mere chaga tincture there is never maximum utilization of the power. Specialized emulsion solves this, rendering all the key sterol substances to be maximally absorbed, especially when taken as sublingual drops. The absorbed sterols will give the cells the power they need for regeneration.

Regarding the chaga expresso this is also regenerative, since a hot water treatment helps liberate the active ingredients from this mushroom and, therefore, assists in sterol absorption. However, for maximum benefit this infusion should be consumed with food rich in natural cholesterol such as organic whole milk and/or yogurt, organic raw or pasteurized cheese, organic/cage-free eggs, and to a degree meat such as grass-fed beef, organic chicken, and organic poultry (keep the skin on with the poultry). The expresso can be consumed with a full meal to take advantage of the chaga sterols. Yet, it can also be consumed on an empty stomach.

This fat/lipid connection is maximized through the intake of a chaga emulsion. Here, wild raw chaga is emulsified in spice oils to create a creamy extract. Taken as drops under the tongue this offers a maximum absorption of the key active ingredients such as betulin, betulinic acid, lanosterol, and lupeol.

Can sterols—and steroids—be consumed from plants?

It is difficult to get all the steroid or steroid-like molecules needed by the body from plants. It might be said that this is the ultimate purpose of edible animals, that is so that humans could procure a concentrated source of invaluable steroid molecules. Again, it is all according to a refined plan.

Yet, why are the steroids so crucial? It is because these molecules are required for the function of dozens of systems in the body. For instance, the coating on the nerve sheaths, including the coating of the nerves of the brain, is derived from cholesterol. This demonstrates the crucial nature of this molecule. The cell walls of all the cells in the body use this wax as a key structural component but also for repairing any damage. Furthermore, the hormone system is dependent upon cholesterol, since this is the raw material used in the production of hormones. It is the hormones which are largely the basis of the body's ability to thrive and also of the capacity to cope—with stress, toxicity, allergy, infection, and more. Hormones that are produced from cholesterol include cortisol, DHEA, aldosterone, progesterone, estrogen, testosterone, and vitamin D to name a few. If levels of these hormones are low, this tells of sterol/steroid deficiency. Thus, the intake of cholesterol-rich food, as well as chaga mushroom and birch bark extract, is indicated. Chaga provides much needed sterols in a highly biologically active form. This is wild-source sterols. Nothing could be more powerful than that.

Stripping cholesterol from the body is highly destructive. It leads to a breakdown in the strength of the cells. It also leads to immune decay as well as degeneration of the nervous system. Additionally, the brain can suffer damage as a result of its deficiency. This organ is largely made of cholesterol.

It is difficult to procure sufficient cholesterol from a plant-based diet. This is because there is no cholesterol in plants. There are instead sterols and sterolins, which are, to a degree, precursors to cholesterol. Yet, some of these sterols and sterolins are antagonists to animal steroids.

In the non-animal kingdom the closest sterols molecularly to animal steroids are those from mushrooms. Thus, emulsified chaga mushroom extract and/or the hot-water infusion offer steroid-like substances which can be readily used by the body and can replace to a degree the need for animal sources. Even so, for ideal health it would be necessary to consume if possible a source of animal steroids, even if it was nothing more than organic eggs, yogurt, and cheese. This will at least provide sufficient steroid molecules for the essential productions of the human body, such as the synthesis of hormones and the creation of the critical myelin sheath, which coats the nerves of the brain and elsewhere.

Thus, chaga mushroom extracts are invaluable nutritionally for the human body. Through their intake essential steroid-like molecules, minerals, enzymes, phenolic compounds, and vitamins are all provided in dense amounts. The same is true of birch bark extracts, which are also whole foods and which were used as actual food by the primitives. For people restricted to plant-based diets the intake of nutrient- and sterol-dense extracts made from tree bark and/or chaga mushroom is essential for optimal health, since these supply a density of nutrients often lacking in the diet. For instance, for vegans the sterols of chaga and birch bark are lifesaving. Other remote-source foods which supply desperately needed nutrients for vegans/vegetarians include the wild raw greens drops, which are a rich source of riboflavin, and raw purple maca extract, which supplies a small amount of B_{12} and vitamin D. Maca and chaga are an excellent combination, since both contain these invaluable nutrients.

Chaga and birch bark sterols: the ultimate protection

The consumption of the aforementioned sterols is no minor issue. These are potent high energy compounds of immense biochemical activity. Without sterols there is no life. If they are even moderately deficient, there is no quality of life. Sterols are biological waxes, known chemically as lipids. As mentioned previously these lipids serve a critical function for cell membranes. This is to prevent degeneration. By preventing degeneration of the cell membranes these substances effectively block the onset of degenerative diseases, particularly cancer, arthritis, diabetes, and heart disease. The premise, here, is that the greater the intake of sterols or sterol-like substances the more powerful is overall health as well as the potential for an increase in lifespan.

The consumption of emulsified chaga and birch bark sterols is the easiest way to retard the aging process. Moreover, these sterols stall the development of heart disease, cancer, and diabetes. Then, their role in blocking the aging process and, therefore, premature death is obvious, since these are the major killers of modern society.

Regarding the increasing of lifespan the anticancer action of chaga sterols alone gives evidence. Moreover, this action is confirmed by orthodox organizations such as the Japanese Cancer Society. Here, medical directors state that in the eradication of cancer chaga plays a crucial role. Then, in modern society this disease is the number two killer, so by stalling this, or curing it, obviously, lifespan will increase.

According to Japanese investigators the chaga sterols enter directly into cancer cells, acting to stabilize their membranes. Incredibly, this prevents cancer from growing excessively and spreading. The society also reports that chaga is an effective therapy when combined with standard cancer treatment, since it speeds the destruction of tumors, while diminishing the side effects of toxic treatments.

Yet, all cells incorporate these sterols. Moreover, stabilization is precisely what the aging body requires. By stabilizing cell membranes the efficiency, as well as lifespan, of human cells can be maximized. This demonstrates the value of taking chaga as a daily or near daily supplement.

Antifungal power

There is little people can do about fungal infections. The drugs often used may exhibit a greater degree of toxicity than the disease itself. The question is what can be done to activate the immune system to purge fungi? Certainly, spice oils are antifungal, that is they directly kill these germs. Yet, still, there is a need to boost the immune system's ability to kill fungi—because for most humans this ability has been fully compromised. It is chaga and birch bark which correct this. This is largely due to their content of antifungal sterols. The sterols are incorporated into the cell walls of fungi. In this regard they weaken them and make these organisms vulnerable to self-destruction. In what is a kind of miracle these sterols simultaneously strengthen the cell membranes of white blood cells, thereby increasing their capacity to kill fungal invaders.

The major antifungal drugs Nizoral, Nystatin, and Amphotericin B, like the chaga/birch bark components, act on the cell walls. So, to have non-toxic substances which do this is a major issue. The sterols in chaga and birch bark achieve precisely this feat. A number of studies, particularly those by Finnish investigator Kahlos, published in *Planta Medica*, have shown that these sterols are highly antifungal. Also, in the 1970s European researchers proved that a key sterol in chaga, inotodiol, which is similar to the steroids in the human body, has both antitumor and antifungal activity. Regardless, since the sterols in birch bark and chaga work via the same mechanism as the drugs it is obvious which ones are the most ideal for human use.

The sterols have a unique mechanism of action that is surely beyond comprehension. This mechanism is proof of intelligent design. Incorporated into the cell walls of fungal cells they cause their death, while when utilized by the walls of healthy human cells, they strengthen them. Moreover, because they are rich in molecular oxygen these substances cause a direct killing action against fungi. The fungi are sensitive to high oxygen environments. In fact, oxygen is one of the most potent fungicides known. Chaga is one of the plant kingdom's most potent source of molecular oxygen.

The power of chaga and birch bark sterols against fungi is subtle. Methodically, they cause the purging of fungal invaders. This is through a direct antifungal effect and also a potent action upon the immune system. The typical sluggish immunity of the body versus fungi is largely reversed as a result of regular chaga and birch bark therapy. Thus, chaga and/or birch bark emulsions made from the raw, wild materials are essential in any antifungal treatment protocol. Fungally-induced diseases which respond to chaga/birch bark therapy include diabetes, histoplasmosis, chronic bronchitis, chronic sinusitis, serous otitis media, chronic pneumonia, blastomycosis, valley fever, alopecia, psoriasis, eczema, vitiligo, candidiasis, and aspergillosis.

How to find the most powerful forest cures

The most powerful forest cures are those which are the least altered. They are also those which are derived from the most remote regions of the forest and wilderness. These are cures in which the true powers of nature are trapped. Largely in the raw state they are preserved and extracted only with natural substances and are, thus, free of all synthetics.

Such natural medicines are produced by only the finest nutritional supplement companies in the world. These are companies which actually send their people into the forests to collect the natural medicines. Then, they manufacture the natural medicines on site in order to trap all their powers. In doing so they do all in their power to avoid disturbing nature and to harvest ethically. Plus, by applying this technique of careful harvesting and the use only of non-toxic methods the medicinal properties of the various plants are preserved. This is particularly true of the raw extracts, which as a consequence of being created without cooking/heat even retain their live enzymes. A list of raw, remote-source forest extracts prepared without the use of chemicals includes wild raw chaga expresso, wild raw emulsified chaga drops, birch bark extract, berries extracts, white birch bark tea, greens extracts, and poplar bud extract.

A sign of quality is the fact that only wild materials are harvested. In addition, in any ingredients wild and organic materials are used. For preservatives, instead of synthetic substances, such as sodium benzoate and sorbic acid, natural and/or wild spice oils are used.

With chaga this is not difficult, because the ideal form is the spice oil and fatty emulsion as well as the birch-bark fortified expresso. These are also ideal, because they are entirely natural, that is they are not extracted with high heat or chemicals. With poplar buds, as well, the most desirable form is an emulsion in a base of raw apple cider vinegar and extra virgin olive oil. Regarding wild greens the key is the intake of a raw extract, ideally containing wild dandelion leaf extract, wild burdock leaf extract, and wild nettles extract. Regarding the wild berries, again, only wild, raw extracts are medicinal. Such extracts will provide the dependable results, as mentioned in this book.

Oyster mushroom: another unique natural medicine

Oyster mushroom is an edible fungus which, like chaga, grows on trees. It is a powerful creation, since it has the ability to digest wood, something that even the powerful digestive tracts of humans cannot achieve. Thus, oyster mushroom is a potent source of enzymes capable of digesting tough matter.

This mushroom is a true whole food with significant medicinal powers. In mice extracts of the mushroom have been determined to be highly medicinal. It is a significant antitumor and antifungal agent. Additionally, this mushroom is a potent cholesterol-lowering agent. One group of researchers called the effect "pronounced" and even alluded that this effect would stall the progression of degenerative changes in the arteries, that is atherosclerosis. In fact, in a study done in Germany published in *Nahrung* (1999) on rabbits the feeding of oyster mushroom as 10% of the diet led to a significant reduction in the number of lesions, as well as the size of these lesions, in the arteries of cholesterol-fed rabbits. Furthermore, this mushroom causes in test animals a reduction in blood sugar. According to Sloan-Kettering Cancer Center the main uses of this whole food are the treatment of cancer, diabetes, high blood fat levels, and infections. The main components of this mushroom are polysaccharides, notably 3-D-beta glucan and pleuran, lectins, peptides, and mevinolin.

Oyster mushroom contains a lectin which has demonstrated antitumor activity in mice bearing sarcoma and hepatoma. This is a significant finding, since, essentially, this lectin acts as a natural chemotherapeutic agent. One of its amino acid groups or peptides, pleurostrin, is a potent antifungal agent. This makes sense, because the mushroom has to protect itself against various molds, which would cause it to rot. Mevinolin is an agent which inhibits enzymes which are involved in cholesterol synthesis. Thus, this is an effective inhibitor of cholesterol production. The beta glucan pleuran is also a significant antitumor agent. One study found that this substance, when fed in significant quantities to mice, 10% of the total feed, caused a significant reduction in precancerous changes in mice colon.

When dealing with natural substances, there is a profound benefit. One of these benefits is the lack of toxicity. For instance, according to the conservative Sloan-Kettering Cancer Center there is no known adverse reaction to the use of oyster mushroom or its extracts in cancer treatment.

In support of these findings according to Indian investigators this mushroom exhibits significant tumor-killing properties. Here, investigators at the Indian Institute of Technology found that oyster mushroom greatly boosted immune function in the fight against cancer.

There are substances also in this mushroom which lower cholesterol. Known as statins these are the same compounds as are found in the common drugs. Oyster mushrooms contain up to 2.7% statins by weight, which is a considerable amount of this cholesterol-blocking agent.

A number of rat studies demonstrate the capacity of oyster mushroom in blocking cancer development, especially cancers induced by exposure to carcinogenic chemicals. In one study the mere addition of dried oyster mushroom to the diets of coal tar-induced colon cancer significantly reduced the degree of cancer pathology in the colon wall. Other studies have demonstrated that fat soluble substances in oyster mushroom, most likely the sterols, exhibit potent cancer-killing properties.

High grade chaga supplements: the role of emulsification

It is well known that with chaga there are challenges in absorption. This is true primarily of the molecularly large sterols. In the crude state absorption of sterols may be as low as one percent. The reason is that sterols are waxes, which are highly difficult to absorb, that is unless a person has ideal digestion. Even then the absorption proves difficult. This is resolved by emulsification. In this process the sterols are mycelized, meaning they are rendered soluble in water. Essentially, they are turned into a cream, which means they are readily taken up by the intestinal membranes and transported into the blood as well as lymph. It is through this means that the person can get the maximum benefits of both chaga and birch bark.

The wild chaga, the birch bark tea, and birch bark expresso are non-emulsified. However, when just boiled water is poured over them, emulsification to a degree occurs. Regardless, this is the traditional way of making chaga extract.

The addition of fat or whole milk to the hot chaga/birch bark drink boosts sterol absorption. In the event of milk allergy this can be achieved by the addition of almond or rice milk or, perhaps, nut oils. Raw honey can also be added, since this also boosts sterol absorption.

The important issue is that the sterols in the raw state are difficult to absorb. Remember, these molecules are waxes, and so under normal circumstances they are virtually impossible to absorb. Imagine the impairment in absorption in a person with compromised digestive function. This may explain the traditional method of consuming chaga as a hot, that is just-boiled, water infusion. It also demonstrates the value of emulsions based upon blended spice oils, which greatly enhances absorption through the gut and also through the skin.

Apoptosis: key mechanism of action

The sterols in birch bark and chaga offer a unique power which accounts for much of their medicinal action. This is the power of apoptosis. It is apoptosis which is the most sure means of curing cancer. The term means "programmed cell death." That's right, the sterols in these medicines cause the cancer cell to program its own self destruction.

This means essentially that the chaga/birch bark sterols are cytotoxic, that is they are destructive—but this destruction is directed only at diseased cells. A number of studies have demonstrated that there is no toxicity against normal cells. The wild chaga and birch bark extracts are not only safe for human consumption, but they are also entirely safe in large quantities: as much as a person desires to consume. This is invaluable for cancer therapy, where it is often necessary to consume massive amounts are often necessary to consume in order to obliterate the tumor(s).

That the sterols are responsible for chaga's and birch bark's destructive action against tumors has been thoroughly confirmed. Consider the first portion of the title of the article in *Pharmacology* starting with "Betulinic acid-induced apoptosis...", in other words, the sterol betulinic acid is the key substance responsible for the destruction of cancer cells. This is incredible considering the negative press that has existed regarding steroids and steroid-like molecules.

So, it is true, cancer and various other diseases of bizarre cell growth are not nearly as incurable as has been presumed. There are natural complexes which aggressively purge such cells. Of these, chaga is perhaps the most sophisticated, although birch bark extract is also exceptional. Because of their rich content of biologically active sterols, particularly betulin and betulinic acid, these extracts are among the most potent anticancer agents known. They are agents of apoptosis, which means that they are a kind of natural chemotherapy.

The apoptosis action is invaluable not merely for cancer but for virtually any disease associated with bizarre cell growth. Thus, this mechanism of action is also a key one for the reversal of psoriasis and eczema. Chaga activates the body's immune system. If the immune system is neutralized, it cannot purge noxious growths, and this includes the growths of cancerous tumors, benign tumors, and inflammatory skin diseases. In all such conditions chaga, as a raw emulsion and hot infusion/expresso, is the treatment of choice. This is because it causes the immune system to eradicate the diseased tissue and also acts directly on such tissue, causing its destruction.

Alertness/mental health

Both wild chaga and white birch bark extract are ideal for mental health. There are several reasons for this. Because of the rich content of sterols these natural medicines strengthen the reserve system. The sterols directly nourish brain and nerve tissue. Plus, these substances nourish the adrenal glands, and these glands exert a major influence over the function of the brain and nerves. By building a stronger nervous system, as well as adrenal system, chaga and birch bark increase mental powers. Thus, it is commonly reported that as a result of the intake of these substances there is a great increase in mental focus and alertness. The stamina of the mind is obviously enhanced, that is there is less tendency for mental fatigue despite the task.

So, chaga can be relied upon to enhance the basic mental functions. When there is a need for a greater alertness, such as during classes, exams, driving, writing, or reading, this mushroom should be consumed, ideally as sublingual drops.

Chaga is also a mild antidepressive, since it activates the energy mechanisms within the neurons. Furthermore, since it exerts a calming action on the body it is also an antianxiety agent. This is in part due to its powers in rehabilitating adrenal function. It is these glands which help maintain normal balance of the nervous system. Chaga is one of the most potent adrenal-balancing foods known.

Cultured mushrooms versus wild: beware of laboratory-made chaga

In medicine there is always the tendency to corrupt nature. This is now being done with chaga. There is an effort to grow this blessed plant in the laboratory. This is done in cell culture, where merely the mycelia or fungal tentacles are grown. Then, these are harvested and used in research.

The problem is the laboratory type is entirely different than the one in the wild. It contains less sterols, plus those which do exist are in a ratio which is completely distorted. Additionally, compared to the natural kind laboratory-grown chaga is more irritating to the body. Yet, the fact that the laboratory type is weaker in power than the wild one is sufficient reason to avoid its use. As mentioned previously one study demonstrated that the synthetic type is up to 1000% different in the ratio of certain steroids than the original/wild type.

People often resist the idea of a plan in nature. Yet, it is true. This world is operated by a great design. The great creator produces wild medicines according to a system. When such wild medicines are used in the original, that is corruption-free, state, the results are dependable. Humans can only experiment. Yet, the important point is that He creates. In contrast, the human being can create nothing and instead can only produce manipulations of whatever exists. Chaga is a complex natural creation that is rare and from the most remote regions. It is a kind of trap of the power of birch trees, so that the compounds of this tree can be utilized medicinally. In this respect it is a vast blessing. Making it synthetically cannot compare to the process required in nature, where the mushroom has to fight for its life. The tree upon which it grows also must fight for its existence. This is entirely different than the process in a lab, where there is no environmental stress. Man-made products may look similar, but, chemically, they are different. The emulsified wild, raw chaga drops and the wild raw chaga expresso are true remote-source natural supplements. Made exclusively from chaga and/or birch bark collected from far northern forests these are entirely free of synthetic components.

Can people be sensitive?

With wild chaga there are few if any precautions. Even so, there is one area for precautionary advice. No matter how safe is chaga, still, it is a fungus. Thus, ideally, chaga should not be used with other potent fungal extracts. For instance, antibiotics are largely made from fungi. The two should not be used together. Furthermore, extracts of chaga and birch bark are mainly for adults. Here, it is safe for various uses and has no negative effect, even in the event of serious disease, liver disorders, or kidney disease.

Even so, there are many arenas where the young could benefit from such chaga's versatility. For children it can be consumed in modest amounts, like a few drops of the raw emulsion daily. A light tea can be made, using about a third the adult dose. In primitive societies chaga tea was commonly consumed by both adults and children. For children with eczema it can also be applied topically, directly from the bottle of emulsified liquid. In the event of childhood allergy to fungi or mushrooms it should be used cautiously or avoided. It may be safely tested by putting one drop under the tongue. If there are no reactions, then, a few drops daily can be consumed. As a rule this is a food-like substance, so there is no toxicity. However, even in the event of mushroom sensitivity for skin disorders it may be used topically. Furthermore, although rare, reactions such as headache can indicate sensitivity to fungi. In such a case the person may halt the intake. To test again merely take one drop under the tongue, and increase the dose by a drop or two daily. If there are no further reactions, then, it may be consumed regularly.

Yet, the point is virtually anyone can tolerate this highly nutritious food, particularly if it is started gradually. In fact, chaga is more well tolerated than the typical food mushrooms. Plus, it is far more dense in nutrients, vitamins, minerals, enzymes, and antioxidants, than such mushrooms.

It bears emphasizing. In China, Russia, Korea, and Japan, as well as much of eastern Europe, chaga mushroom is a traditional remedy. Here, it is often used routinely. There is no record of toxicity and/or side effects in all this usage. Thus, in fact, chaga is the safest of all mushroom extracts for human use.

As a proof of the power of sterols in human health consider the following testimony. True, it is not total proof; however, it is surely inviting. Says one native observer, "My grandparents are Maine Penobscot, Native Americans, and drink chaga tea every day. They are aged 102 and 105 and are still very healthy. They attribute health and long life to the chaga." Perhaps they are correct.

Chapter Nine

Sunlight: the Power of Color

It is now proven that the real power in nature is derived from the sun. If a plant can cure, it is because it provides sunlight power. This is in the form of photons, which are high energy molecules. Plants trap these molecules, and if the plant or plant extract is intact, in other words, if it is not heated, then the power remains. That power can be identified through the color of the plant. Any deep intense color is a sign of high photon energy.

For this reason all the natural medicines described in this book are in a raw form. This maximizes the healing powers. When heat is applied, especially prolonged heat, the photons are dissipated, that is they are lost. However, if the raw supplement is immersed in hot or just boiled water, much of this photon energy is retained. An even more biologically potent form is produced when the raw material is immersed in cool water and consumed immediately. The forests are full of color. the prominent colors are greens, reds, ochres, yellows, oranges, reddish browns, and violets. All such colors are medicinal.

There is great power in color. People should select food based upon this. Obviously, some of the most beautifully colored plants, fruits, and vegetables are also the most medicinal. When viewing a forest, everyone is struck by the beautiful representation of color. This is a representation of energy in the form of the sun, specifically in the form of photons.

For ideal power in harvesting any forest cure great care must be taken. Here, the color must be retained. This means the powers of the forest medicines are captured and thus available for human benefit. This is achieved through careful conscientious harvesting of exclusively wild material. Such material is sun-charged—and as long as it isn't treated with excessive amounts of heat and/or noxious chemicals this sun-charge remains in the final material. As noted by Scott in *Health, Diet, and Common Sense* color is curative. He quotes the work of Indian scholars who found that trapped sunlight, when applied in this case through sunlight trapped in colored bottles, has enormous powers against disease. Disease, noted the early Indian investigators, is a deficiency "of a certain color in the human system."

An Indian book called *Chromopathy* advocates the use of color-charged water in the treatment of a wide range of diseases. Berries, rich in color, are now known to gain their powers from their electrical charges, and these charges are held within the molecules, the flavonoids and polyphenols, which are responsible for their color. It is not so absurd, says Scott, especially when considering the fact that color is a vibrational power, and it is well known in medicine that vibrational energy can speed the healing process.

Another color investigator was Madame de Chrapowicki, the author of *Spectro-Biology*, who used color therapy against disease. According to Scott the therapy was highly effective "against a great many and varied diseases…"

Chaplin made a chart describing the specificity of certain colors in disease treatment. Here is what he determined:

Green: fights inflammation and reverses nervous strain; acts as a relaxant

Blue: fights infection and reverses anemia

Yellow: stimulates the brain

Orange: acts to stimulate physical strength and also balances emotions

Red/rose: same as orange

Purple (violet): acts on the heart, lungs, and blood vessels

All the forest cures are highly colored. Moreover, again, that is a mere reflection and is due to the spectrum of color from sunlight. Again, this sunlight energy is trapped in the plant chemicals. Sumac is reddish-purple, rose hips, when pulverized, are yellowish-orange, tamarack is brown with a hint of violet, birch bark is yellowish-white, while chaga is a rich orange-brown. Of note, both tamarack and sumac have significant use in the treatment of arterial and heart diseases. Both are purplish in tone. Rose hips, which are orange, have long been used as a strength tonic, especially in the winter. The tips of pine, tamarack, and fir trees, which are green, contain potent antiinflammatory compounds. There are also the wild forest greens, as a raw triple greens complex (greens flushing agent), which greatly reduce inflammation in the intestinal canal. Regarding chaga there is no doubt that this orange-brown complex is one of the most potent inducers of physical strength known. Thus, it would appear that the early color investigators are correct. People love the color of the forest. It is one of the human being's greatest dreams to be surrounded among a peaceful forest, with verdant green and lush plant growth. People find peace in such a surrounding and crave the feeling of restoration that it provides.

The remedies described in this book are powerful because they are rich in photonic energy. So, they are correspondingly rich in color. Without color there is no power. When found in the wilderness, chaga has a black-colored exterior and an orange-brown interior. Birch bark is a beautiful white on the outside, while orange-brown internally. Regarding wild berries they range usually in various shades of red and blue. The black color of blackberries and black raspberries is nothing more than an intense form of red. Blueberries are an intense blue, sometimes covered with a soft white blush. Acai, the tropical berry, is a purplish-red, while black raspberry is such a deep purple that it appears black. Rose hips are a pinkish-red on the outside, but when pulverized become a beautiful orange color with hints of yellow and a bit of red. Sumac is a deep crimson or purplish-red. Tamarack bark is a kind of purplish-brown.

All these colors merely represent the sun. This is because what people see isn't really as it appears. Rather, it is merely the vibrations which are being sensed. The sensors are the human retina. This organ detects the vibrations which emanate from the plants. The vibrations represent stored energy in the plant systems. When these plants are harvested, this energy is largely retained, that is if the harvested material is kept in a raw state free of corruption. The corruption comes in the form of noxious chemicals, which are commonly used to extract herbs and other plant matter. All such chemicals, or solvents, destroy the original vibratory energy. A list of high energy, high vibration food supplements, where the photonic power is intact include the following, which are categorized by their healing color:

High vibrational supplements

Green
- mega-dose wild, raw Mediterranean-source oregano tea (pulverized)
- soothing wild, raw Mediterranean-source sage tea (pulverized)
- sweet wild, raw hyssop tea (pulverized)
- wild, raw triple greens flushing agent

Blue
- wild, raw blueberry extract (as sublingual drops)

Yellow/ochre
- wild, raw yarrow tea (pulverized)
- wild, raw birch bark tea (pulverized)
- wild, raw oyster mushroom

Orange/brown
- wild, raw chaga mushroom (pulverized)
- wild, raw rose hips tea (pulverized)

Red
- wild, raw and remote-source raw strawberry extract (as a beverage - see Americanwildfoods.com)
- wild, raw lingonberry extract (as sublingual drops)
- wild, raw red raspberry extract (as sublingual drops)
- wild, raw sumac tea (pulverized)

Purple/violet
- wild, raw blackberry extract (as sublingual drops)
- wild, raw black raspberry extract (as sublingual drops)
- wild, raw tamarack (larch) bark tea (pulverized)

Note: match the color of these healing complexes with the previous chart giving the specific curative properties. For instance, rose hips are orange-to-rosey and thus give strength to the body and the brain, while black raspberry, which is purple, enhances the function of the blood and blood vessels. Regarding the latter extracts of this fruit have been show, when kept in the raw state, to destroy tumors. This is through the effect of the black raspberry extract on a phenomenon known as angiogenesis, which means aberrant blood vessel growth. Black raspberry extract (Rubus species) cause a normalization of blood vessel development thereby cutting off the blow to tumors.

Regarding chaga this is a yellowish- or orange-brown. Thus, true to form this greatly enhances the health of the brain and physical body. Tamarack, which is purple, strengthens the heart. Thus, the color cure is real.

The vibratory energy, when intact, is noted by the color intensity of the final substance. If the health supplement is of the highest quality, rich in vibratory energy, it will have a rich color. That color will appear also rich/vibrant when the supplement is added to water or food. The colors of the forest are a sign of immense powerful vibrational energy, if only humans will realize it.

Chapter Ten

Conclusion

Medicines in this world which can regenerate the body are rare. This is particularly true when the body and tissues have degenerated due to neglect or poor diet. As well, what is left in this world which can regenerate the body, once it has degenerated as a result of toxicity and/or self-destruction? What exists which can revive people after their systems have failed? What can cause people who are no longer able to function, who have no real energy or vitality, to become regenerated with all the energy they need? It is only the forest cures derived from medicinal trees which can do so. Moreover, this makes sense. Any natural substances or complexes which are powerful enough to keep alive massive beings—well-rooted and tall trees—are surely the most powerful medicines for humans.

With forest cures the results are rapid and dependable. Like other plants, trees must make substances for their survival. It is just that these tree substances, such as betulin and betulinic acid, are more intense, that is more vigorous, than those of tinier plants. Trees must withstand the stresses of pollution, harsh weather, bright sunlight, and pestilence. It is the chemicals which they produce which cause them to do so.

When these natural chemicals are ingested by humans, they do gain the benefits not only of fighting stress but also fighting disease.

There is great science behind this. In the bibliography of this book a number of scientific studies have been listed— and these are studies conducted by researchers all over the world. None of the science is equivocal, that is borderline. As with any other medicine it either works, or it has no effect— or the effect is marginal. In the case of tree medicine, especially chaga and birch bark extracts, there is no doubt about the effects. They are definite, provable, and powerful.

Then, what does the science show? Regarding chaga and white birch bark it shows that there is a definite anticancer effect against a wide range of tumors. Additionally, it shows that, clearly, there is a generalized antiinflammatory action as well as an action for simultaneously normalizing the immune system. Too, it shows that in the event of serious disease, such as cancer and tuberculosis, there is an effect on activating the immune system. As well, these natural medicines have a degree of antiseptic power, that is they directly kill germs. There is also an action of both chaga and birch bark on the circulatory system, where overall function is improved and where there is regeneration, particularly of the heart muscle and arterial walls.

This means that chaga and birch bark extracts are essential natural medicines for the treatment of immune disorders, cancer, as well as those with a vulnerability to cancer, arterial disease, and heart disease. Then, if the circulatory system and immune system are normalized through the intake of such a substance, what more could be desired? Chaga's power in reducing the incidence of tuberculosis, heart disease, arterial disease, diabetes, and cancer alone is sufficient reason to consume it. Thus, surely, those who proclaim it as a longevity aid are correct. Any substance with such broad effects will help people a longer and more vital life.

With the buds of wild trees there is also power. These buds are the seeds for future growth. Thus, they concentrate the trees' greatest powers. The buds of poplar trees have been used for thousands of years medicinally. They are the basis of the ancient formula known as Balm of Gilead. This balm was also known as Meccan balsam. For centuries this has been used topically for the reversal of inflammation and injury. The discoveries, here, are that it has great power also when taken internally. The most powerful type of buds are from far northern trees, where there is the challenge of extreme weather. This forces the plants to produce a greater amount and potency of protective phytochemicals, which are concentrated in the buds. Studies show that the buds and preferably their extract are highly antiinflammatory, both topically and internally, as well as germicidal. For best results both the tree bark medicines and the bud extracts may be taken. Even so, the raw, wild poplar bud extract is particularly valuable for arthritis and other forms of chronic pain. It is also a key natural medicine for inflammatory disorders of the skin such as psoriasis and eczema. Poplar buds are the basis of one of the most renowned natural medicines of the world, which is bee propolis.

Other important forest medicines are wild berries and their extracts. Too, the science has confirmed their powers, notably the ability of berry flavonoids to cause destruction of cancer cells and also their ability to regenerate the circulatory system. Also, the wild berry extracts are documented starch blockers, which means they assist in the mobilization of abdominal fat. In cancer for ideal results the chaga/birch bark extracts must always be combined with wild, raw berries extracts.

Regardless, it is not easy to be a tree. All sorts of forces attempt to attack it. There is the force of the wind, which attempts to bring the tree down. The sun is a powerful force, which, if it were not for the tree's protective chemicals, would scorch it. Too, the temperature, too hot or cold, would, were it not for its protective forces, destroy it. The same is true of pests. For trees the challenge is every conceivable creature attempts to feed off them. The reason they are not eaten up by such invaders is because of the natural protective chemicals they synthesize. Thus, humans can gain great power by consuming natural medicines derived from the edible portions of trees. Additionally, the various fungi which grow on these edible portions are also key medicines, as they concentrate the therapeutic powers.

In this book the use of miraculous substances from the far northern forests is described. Even for the most hopeless person these will provide benefits. Moreover, they are non-toxic and, thus, can be consumed with impunity. All of the natural medicines described in this book can be taken daily. Barring the occasional but rare allergy none have any toxicity. Nor do any of these natural complexes have any untoward interactions with drugs. Rather, the only 'side effects' are an improvement in overall health and improved appearance. Another side or, rather, additional effect is the prevention of degenerative disease.

With forest cures, particularly the emulsified chaga extract and the chaga/birch bark expresso, the results are obvious. Moreover, these results occur quickly. These results/benefits include an enhanced sense of well being, increased energy, increased vital power, improved vision, increased physical strength, enhanced alertness, improved circulation, and a tremendously enhanced immune system. Routinely, from the intake of this natural medicine people arise more vigorously in the morning and usually arise earlier. Moreover, the increase in physical prowess is significant, because of the fact that through the ingestion of this mushroom there is a desire for muscular work. This is one of the few substances in this world that creates such an intense degree of muscular energy.

There is nothing else like this in this world. In fact, the energy derived from the intake of such a wild, natural food is enormous, as is demonstrated by the reports of those who have taken it. In interviewing these people they have given reports such as "I have never felt this good before," and "I was skeptical, but after taking it I became more energized and alert." One person reported that he now automatically has the energy to do all manner of chores around the home, whereas prior to chaga he procrastinated. Yet another, the wife of a pharmacist, who was plagued with a kind of chronic fatigue, states that "She has never felt so well" and that she "just feels stronger."

Other reports include a reduction in arthritic pain, modest lowering of high blood pressure, reduction in symptoms of spastic colon, better sleep, enhanced immunity, and healthier skin. While this sounds like a "cure-all" it would not be a surprise that chaga could achieve it. This is because this complex is one of the most potent sources of nutrition known. In addition, it effectively activate, rather, strengthens the immune system. Furthermore, it is the world's top source of the highly versatile antioxidant enzyme SOD, plus it is rich in the immune potentiator beta glucan. This is more than sufficient reason to account for its wide ranging effects.

There are people who seek to get well at any price. Moreover, if an opportunity arises for health improvement, such people will rise to the occasion. They will do whatever is necessary to get well. There are others who won't do so and instead want to be 'cared for.' These are the ones who are usually hesitant to do the unorthodox. They might even believe that they could harm themselves with intelligently produced natural medicines—while in the epitome of irrationality they show no concern for taking poisonous drugs. Nor do they hesitate to undergo highly risky surgical procedures, even though they may be largely experimental. They also subject themselves to risky tests, while giving it no thought.

Yet, the forest has always been a key source of the earliest medicines. Aspirin is a prominent example, since this was originally derived from the bark of the white willow tree. So, now it is time to return to this source. There is surely the highly rare chaga, which is forest-derived, but there is also the more readily available wild rose hips and sumac, which offer their own unique medicinal benefits.

The data doesn't lie. In the United States alone every year there are over a half million people who suffer premature death from medical therapies. Surgery, dangerous tests, drugs, and injections all kill. In contrast, it is difficult to confirm even a single case of fatality in this same land from medicinal edible mushrooms, wild-source herbs, natural spices or their extracts, and medicinal roots, not merely in a year but, rather, in a decade. It is even difficult to confirm a single death from any such natural medicines in a century. Yet, let us be conservative and consider merely a year. Four hundred thousands deaths compared to zero? Is there any need for further discussion? Additionally, is not the need for the widespread use of natural medicine now confirmed?

Through what other means can cautious people be convinced? Do such people who refuse to take appropriate natural medicines, while freely taking pharmaceutic drugs: do they have death wishes? Perhaps, they are frightened and feel that the doctors are saviors. So, such people would never do anything for themselves, unless their doctors "approve." They would be afraid to even take a few drops of a natural herbal tincture without getting authorization.

Yes, it is fear that accounts for peoples' reactions. Otherwise, it makes no sense, that is why people wouldn't do all in their power to use the safest means possible to correct their conditions, whether natural or otherwise. Moreover, why people would purposely harm themselves through the intake of known poisons is even more unfathomable.

A person is sick. Instead of using natural, non-toxic medicines—which are actually foods—such a one submits to taking toxins and, thus, becomes even sicker. It must be fear—or a lack of trust. There can be no other explanation.

Regarding nature this is systematic creation. Through the mercy of the creator there are time-tested cures, which are not only effective but are also harmless. Chaga and birch bark are among these. There are also the food-like cures such as wild, raw berries and wild, raw greens. Such foods are designed for human use. So, food-like medicines, for instance, garlic, onions, basil, sage, cumin, oregano, birch bark, chaga, and honey, are entirely safe for human consumption. Barring food allergy there is no way food-based medicines, such as those made from fruit, vegetables, wild greens, wild berries, natural roots, and wild mushrooms, can poison anyone. Nor can such substances/foods seriously interact with any medication. People who worry about this are truly wasting their time.

Thus, chaga is a food, and so is birch bark. People can take these on a daily basis. As has been mentioned it was used as a kind of tea or coffee by the Siberians. This brew was apparently the one which cured one of the world's most famous authors, Alexander Solzhenitsyn, of stomach cancer. He was so impressed by this that this Nobel laureate wrote a kind of autobiography about his struggle with cancer called *Cancer Ward*, in which his experience with chaga is described. The food value of wild birch bark is also well established. For centuries it was used by Native Americans as a survival food and, when well ground, was added to other wild foods in the making of a kind of bread.

There is also much human use of chaga in life-threatening diseases. This human use is supported by major national institutions. In Russia, 1955, this mushroom was approved by the Russian Medical Academy for cancer treatment and became a standard part of the cancer therapy regimen, while according to the National Cancer Institute chaga was used successfully in Australia to treat cancer. Solzhenitsyn found this to be true, so he wrote an entire book about, albeit in novel form. The novel describes a country doctor who believes the low incidence of cancer in Russian peasants is because they regularly consume chaga tea. The patients of the cancer ward who were of peasant background would secretly bring chaga for self-treatment. Moreover, let us not forget. On the mummified remains of "Otzi the Iceman," a corpse some 5300 years old, was found dried chaga. Researchers believe that this mushroom was used extensively at that time in the treatment of viral and bacterial infections as well as to treat intestinal parasites. It was also used, they believe, to prevent viral and bacterial infections. With the decline in peoples' immune systems this may prove to be one of its best uses today.

The safety of natural medicines is beyond question. This is especially true of those which were traditionally used by the primitives. The studies have already been done, which is the prolonged use by native societies. With their original natural medicines they thrived. Without them they degenerated. Yet, even so with many of these medicines a wide range of scientific studies have been performed, which confirm the primitive use. The studies have even found additional uses of which the primitives were unaware.

The folk use alone of chaga is sufficient basis for its use. This folk use is primarily in Russia, where this mushroom is mentioned in Russian classical literature, medical books, monographs, herbal books, and encyclopedias. It is also in eastern Europe, particularly Poland, where chaga has an extensive history for use against stomach conditions and cancer. In contrast, in America there is no early recorded use of chaga. Notes Alma R. Hutchens in her highly touted book *A Handbook of Native American Herbs* "Folk medicine of European Russia and Siberia gives nearly unlimited credit to chaga, which for generations has been thought of as magical." In fact, it is magical that any substance could cause the body to regenerate and, thus, rid itself of its burdens. In most people chaga is capable of achieving this regeneration in a matter of weeks. Believe it, this potent medicine has the power to revive people, even those in a hopeless state.

Yet, its status is elevated further by Russian medicine, where in the 1950s in the main medical centers chaga was standard therapy for cancer. Here, with extract of chaga cancers of the breast, lung, cervix, and stomach were routinely and successfully treated. In 1963 a medical report was published by the Russian government, where chaga mushroom was listed as "recommended" for the treatment of cancers. It is still used today as an adjunct to standard cancer therapy.

Yet, can the intake of chaga and other forest cures prevent this disease? Most people may not have active cancer, but in modern society they largely have the beginnings of it. For instance, should chaga be taken routinely? The data indicates this, for example, the study done in 2008 by Korean investigators. Here, it was shown that chaga "strongly inhibited" damage to chromosomes caused by toxic chemicals. All humans could benefit from such a blockade, since this damage is the precursor to cancer and numerous other diseases. Thus, Korean investigators also proved that this mushroom protects against the typical DNA damage that may lead to diabetes. Clearly, chaga is a preventive against all diseases of civilization.

It is difficult to find a substance in this world as comprehensive as chaga. White birch bark extract is also highly comprehensive. As demonstrated by European investigators these mushroom/bark extracts may be taken with impunity. Poplar bud extract has its own special attributes, largely in the arena of pain and inflammation. Yet, this extract is also a powerful germicide and antitumor agent. All such tree medicines were used for thousands of years by the native residents of Europe and North America. Thus, with raw tree bark/bud extracts the only potential effects are positive.

The science fully supports the medicinal use of these extracts. What had never before been achieved was to make the raw materials absorbable. This has been accomplished through emulsification.

The data on chaga in particular is categorical. Extracts of this mushroom are a source of great physical power. Such extracts greatly empower the immune system in its fight against disease. In particular, clearly, chaga is of immense value versus cancer. It also helps reverse neurological diseases, diabetes, fibromyalgia, and chronic fatigue syndrome. The research shows that chaga is potent in the reversal of diabetes, prostate cancer, lung cancer, stomach cancer, inflammation, muscle atrophy, high cholesterol levels, atherosclerosis, and cancer in general. For support of this note the voluminous references cited at the end of this book.

That great power of wild and remote-source trees is thoroughly established. In the form of highly absorbable emulsions, as well as hot teas, these powers can be concentrated for human use. Regarding all forest cures it is the wild birch bark and the tree mushroom which are most medicinal. These concentrate the vastly powerful medicines of the trees, so they are ready for human use. The key natural medicines are in the form of wild, raw chaga mushroom, white birch bark, tamarack bark, and poplar bud emulsions, as well as pulverized rose hips.

There are many forms of chaga mushroom which are available. However, there is great benefit in consuming chaga and birch bark in a raw, unprocessed state. This can be achieved through the intake of the raw, wild substance, as emulsified sublingual drops. With chaga other forms include boiled and then dried powders, as tea or drops, and the tasty and synergistic expresso or tea made from wild, raw chaga and wild, raw birch bark. In the raw state all the enzymes are intact and the various immune potentiators in the mushroom offer their greatest power. The intake of the expresso in hot water still offers a raw-like effect, although the true raw type is the emulsified drops.

There is no doubt that chaga mushroom is a great blessing. People must gain its benefits ideally from the raw form or the raw material added to just boiled water. This is the most potent and efficient way to consume it. Again, the emulsion is ideal, since, it is raw and is taken in a form for immediate absorption, which is sublingual drops. Regarding rose hips the ideal form is a pulverized powder made from remote-source wild fruit, which is hand harvested. The same is true of sumac, which is most potent when harvested from the far northern regions of America. Tamarack is another natural medicine which must be remotely harvested from far northern regions, because of the ill effects of pollution, the toxins of which are absorbed by the trees. For guaranteed remote-source chaga mushroom extract, chaga expresso, pulverized rose hips, pulverized sumac, sumac lemonade (Sumanade), pulverized tamarack bark, and pulverized birch bark see Americanwildfoods.com. Also, all such natural medicines may be ordered from high quality health food stores.

Without doubt, in all natural medicines chaga is unique. The Chinese called it the King of Plants for no small reason. Nor were the Siberian Russians mincing words when they deemed it "Gift from God" as well as "Mushroom of Immortality." People should take advantage of it for better health. Also, just like Solzhenitsyn, they should do so in the attempt to reverse potentially fatal disease. This is the forest cure premise, which is that through the use of these blessed medicines lives will be saved.

Like any other medicine wild chaga is a limited resource. It can't be grown. Thus, could the demand outstrip the supply? This is surely possible. It takes several years for a chaga to form, in some cases a decade or longer. As it is a repair mechanism for trees, obviously, it's not renewable. Thus, it is truly rare. That is why any dose of this mushroom should be cherished. Now, it is time to take advantage of this power for better health as well as for a long and vigorous life. This positive, safe, and effective power of forest cures is all for human benefit. This is from the grace of the high God who has placed natural medicines on this earth for the benefit of human health. So, take advantage of it and feel the difference. That is the forest cure guarantee.

Bibliography

Anonymous. 2004. Cytotoxic effect of *Inonotus obliquus* composition in HCT-15 human colon and AGS gastric cancer cells. *Journal of the Korean Society of Food Science and Nutrition*. 33:633-640.

Alves, R. E., et al. 2002. Camu camu (*Myrciaria dubia* Mc Vaugh): a rich natural source of vitamin C. *Proc. Interamer. Soc. Trop. Hort.* 46:11-13.

Ajith, T. A. and K. K. Janardhanan. 2007. Indian medicinal mushrooms as a source of antioxidant and antitumor agents. *J. Clin. Biochem. Nutr.* 40:157.

Babitskaya, V. G,, Scherba, V. V., Ikonnikova, N.V., Bisko, N.A., and N.Y. Mitropoiskaya. 2002. Melanin complex from medicinal mushroom *Inonotus obliquus* (Pers:Fr.) Pilat (Chaga) (Aphyllophoromycetidae). *Int. J. Med. Mushrooms*. 4:139-45.

Bobek, P., Ozdin, L., and I. Kajaba. 1997. Dose-dependent hypocholesterolemic effect of oyster mushroom (*Pleurotus ostreatus*) in rats. *Physiol Res*. 47:327-329.

Bobek, P. and S. Galbavy. 1999. Hypocholesteremic and antiatherogenic effect of oyster mushroom (*Pleurotus osteratus*) in rabbits. *Nahrung*. 43:339-342.

Burczyk, J., Gawron, A. Slotwinska, M., Smietana, B., and K. Terminiska. 1996. Antimitotic activity of aqueous extracts of Inonotus obliquus. *Boll. Chim. Farm*. 135:306.

Chang, S. T. 1999. Global impact edible and medicinal mushrooms on human welfare in the 21st century: non-green evolution. *Int. J. Med. Mushr*. 1:1-7.

Chen, C., Zheng, W., Gao, X., Xiang, X., Sun, D., Wei, J., and C. Chu. 2007. Aqueous extract of *Inonotus obliquus* (Fr.) pilat (Hymenochaetaceae) significantly inhibits the growth of sarcoma 180 by inducing apoptosis. *American Journal of Pharmacology and Toxicology*. 2:10-17.

Chihara, G., Maeda, Y., Sasaki, T. and F. Fukuoaka. 1969. Inhibition of mouse sarcoma 180 by polysaccharides from Letin us eodes (Berk.) *Nature*. 222:687.

Chorvathova, V., et al. 1993. Effect of oyster fungus on glycemia and cholesterolaemia in rats with insluin-dependent diabetes. *Physiol. Res.* 42:175-179.

Cui, Yo, Kim, D. S., and K. C. Park. 2005. Antioxidant effects of *Inonotus Oblique. J. Ethnopharmacol.* 96:79-85.

de Sa, M. S., et al. 2009. Antimalarial activity of betulinic acid and derivatives in vitro against *Plasmodium falciprum* and in vivo in P. Berghel-infected mice. *Parisitol. Res.* Jul;105:275-279.

Fulda, S, et al. 1997. Betulinic acid triggers CD95 (APO-1/Fas)- and p53-independent apoptosis via activation of capases in neuroectodermal tumors. *Cancer Research.* 57:4956.

Fulda, S. 2008. Betulinic acid for cancer treatment and prevention. *Int. J. Mol. Sci.* 9:1096-1107.

Fulda, S., Jeremias, I., Pietsch, T. and K. M. Debatin. Betulinic acid: a new chemotherapeutic agent in the treatment of neuroectodermal tumors. *Klin Padiatr.* 211:319-322.

Gu, Y. and S. Gowsala. 2006. Cytotoxic effect of oyster mushroom *Pleurotus ostreatus* on human androgen-independent prostate cancer PC-3 cells. *J. Med. Food.* 9:196-204.

Ham, S. S., et al. 2003. Antimutagenic and cytotoxic effects of ethanol extract from the *Inonotus obliquus. J. Korean Soc. Food Sci. Nutr.* 32:1088-94.

Hawksworth, D. L. 2001. Mushrooms: the extent of the unexplored potential. *Int. J. Med. Mushr.* 2:1-9.

Hossain, S., et al. 2003. Dietary mushroom (Pleurotus ostreatus) ameliorates atherogenic lipid in hypercholesterolaemic rats. *Clin. Exp. Pharmacol. Physiol.* 30:470-475.

Hyun, K. W., Jeong, S. C., Lee, D. H., Park, J. S., and J. S. Lee. 1996. Isolation and characterization of a novel platelet aggregation inhibitory peptide from the medicinal mushroom, Inonotus obliquus. *Boll. Chim. Farm.* 135:306-309.

In-Kyoung, L., Young-Sook, K., Yoon-Woo, J., Jin-Young, J., and Y. Bong-Suk. 2007. New antioxidant polyphenols from the medicinal mushroom *Inonotus obliquus*. *Bioorganic & Medicinal Chemistry Letters*. 17:6678-6681.

Jeremias, I., et al. 2004. Cell death induction by betulinic acid, ceramide, and TRAIL in primary glioblastoma multiforme cells. *Acta Neurochirurgica*. 146:721-729.

Kahlos, K., Kangas, L., and R. Hiltunen. 1987. Antitumor activity of some compounds and fractions from an n-hexane extract of *Inonotus obliquus* in vitro. *Acta Pharm. Fennica*. 96:33-40.

Kharazmi, A. 2008. Laboratory and preclinical studies on the anti-inflammatory and anti-oxidant properties of rosehip powder—identification and characterization of the active component GOPO. *Osteoarhritis and Cartilage*. 16:55-57.

Kim, B. K., Shin, G.G., Jeong, B.S., and J.Y. Cha. 2001. Cholesterol lowering effect of mushrooms powder in hyperlipidemic rats. *J. Korean Soc. Food Sci. Nutr.* 30:510-515.

Kim, Y. O., et al. 2005. Immuno-stimulatory effect of the endopolysaccharide produced by submerged culture of *Inonotus obliquus*. *Life Sci*. 77:2438-56.

Kim, Y. O., et al. 2006. Anti-cancer effect and structural characterization of endo-polysaccharide from cultivated mycelia of *Inonotus obliquus*. *Life Sci*. 79:72-80.

Koyama, T., Yeunhwa, G., and T. Akira. 2008. Fungal medicine, *Fuscoporia obliqua*, as a traditional herbal medicine, in vivo testing and medicinal effects. *Asian Biomedicine*. 2:459-469.

Kraus-Zaki, J. 1957. (In Polish) ACTH jako czynnuk hydrolizujacy kwasy dezoksyrybonukleinowe w zastosowaniu do bada cytoenzymatycznych. *Haematologica.* 1:48-50.

Krauss-Zaki, J. 1962. Correspondence: Digestion of Cell Nucleus by Enzymes. *Blood Journal.* 19:527.

Lindequist, U., Niedermeyer, T. H. J., and W-D Julich. 2005. The pharmacological potential of mushrooms. Institute of Pharmacy, Greifswald, Germany.

Lull, C., Wichers, H. J., and H. F. J. Savelkoul. 2005. Antiinflammatory and immunomodulating properties of fungal metabolites (In) Mediators of Inflammation. Hindawi Publishing Corp.

McCord, J. M. and I. Fridovich. 1988. Superoxide dismutase: the first twenty years (1968-1988). *Free Radic. Biol. Med.* 5(5-6):363-369.

Mizuno, T., et al. 1999. Antitumor and hypoglycemic activities of polysaccharides from Sclerotia and mycelia of *Inonotus obliquus. Int. J. Med. Mushrooms.* 1:306.

Mizuno, T. 1999. The extraction and development of antitumor-active polysaccharides from medicinal mushrooms in Japan (review). *Int. J. Med. Mushr.* 1:9-30.

Mothana, R. A. A., Awadh, N. A. A., Jansen, R., Wegner, U., Mentel, R., and U. Lindequist. 2003. Antiviral lanostanoid triterpenes from the fungus *Ganoderma pfeifferi* BRES *Fitoteraia.* 74:483-485.

Mullauer, F. B., Kessler, J. H., and J. P. Medema. Betulin is a potent anti-tumor agent that is enhanced by cholesterol. 2009. (by) Laboratory for *Experimental Oncology and Radiology*, PLoS One; 4(4).

Muller, F. L., et al. 2006. Absence of CuZn superoxide dismutase leads to elevated oxidative stress and acceleration of age-dependent skeletal muscle atrophy. *Free Radic. Biol. Med.* 40:1993-2004.

Najafzadeh, M., et al. 2007. Chaga mushroom extract inhibits oxidative DNA damage in lymphocytes of patients. *Biofactors.* 31:191-200.

Nakagawa-Goto, K., Taniguchi, M., Tokuda, H., and K. H. Lee. 2008. Cancer preventive agents 9. Betulinic acid derivatives as potent cancer chemopreventive agents. *Bioorg. Med. Chem. Lett.* 1;19:3378-3381.

Nasar-Abbas, S. M. and A. Kadir Haikman. 2004. Antimicrobial effect of water extract of sumac (Rhus coriaria L.) on the growth of some food borne bacteria, including pathogens. *J. Food Micro.* 10:1016.

Nicolson, G. L., et al. 2000. Diagnosis and integrative treatment of intercelluar bacterial infections in chronic fatigue and fibromyalgia syndromes, Gulf War Illness, and rheumatoid arthritis and other chronic illnesses. *Clin. Prac. Alt. Med.* 1:92.

Nicolson, G. L. 2002. Co-infections in fibromyalgia syndrome, chronic fatigue syndrome, and other chronic illnesses. *National Fibromyalgia Partnership—Fibromyalgia Frontiers.* 10:5-9; 27-28.

Papas, A. M. (ed). 1999. *Anitoxidant Status, Diet, Nutrition, and Health.* Boca Raton: CRC Press.

Park, Y. M., et al. 2005. In vivo and in vitro anti-inflammatory and anti-nociceptive effects of the methanol extract of *Inonotus obliquus. J. Ethnopharmacol.* 101:120-128.

Park, Y. M., et al. 2007. In vivo and in vitro anti-inflammatory and anti-nociceptive effects of the methanol extract of *Inonotus obliquus. J. Med. Food.* 10:80-90.

Rein, E., Kharazmi, A., and K. Winther. 2004. A herbal remedy, Hyben Vital (stand. Powder of Rosa canina fruits) reduces pain and improves general welbeing in patients with osteoarthritis- a double-blind, placebo controlled randomized trial. *Phytomedicine.* 11:383.

Rzymowska, J. 1996. The effect of aqueous extracts from *Inonotus obliquus* on the mitotic index and enzyme activities. *Boll Chim. Farm.* 135:306-309.

Sarkar, F. H. and Y. Li. 2006. Using chemoprevention agents to enhance the efficacy of cancer therapy. *Cancer Res.* 66:3347.

Sawada, N., et al. 2004. Betulinic acid augments the inhibitory effects of vincristine on growth and lung metastasis of B16F10 melanoma cells in mice. *British Cancer Journal.* 90:1672.

Scott, Cyril. 1944. *Health, Diet, and Common Sense.* London: the Homeopathic Publishing Co.

Shin, Y., Tamai, Y., and M. Terazawa. 2000. Chemical constituents of Inonotus obliquus sclerotium. *Eurasian Journal of Forest Research.* 1:43-50.

Shivrina, A.N. 1967. Chemical characteristics of compounds extracted from *Inonotus obliquus*. *Chem. Abstr.* 66:17271-17279.

Sudhakar, C., Sabitha, P., Shashi, K. R. and S. Safe. 2007. Betulinic acid inhibits prostate cancer growth through inhibition of specificity protein transcription factors. *Cancer Research.* 67:2816.

Sung, B., et al. 2008. Identification of a novel blocker of IkappaBalpha kinase activation that enhances apoptosis and inhibits proliferation and invasion by suppressing nuclear factor-kappaB. *Mol. Cancer Ther.* 7:19-201.

Takada, Y. and B. B. Aggarawal. 2003. Betulinic acid suppresses carcinogen-induced NF-kB activation through inhibition of IkappaB alpha kinase and p65 phosphorylation: abrogation of cyclooxygenase-2 and matrix metalloprotease-9. *Journal of Immunology.* 171:3278.

Wang, H., Gao, J., and T. B. Ng. 2000. A new lectin with highly potent antihepatoma and antisarcoma activities from the oyster mushroom Pleurotus ostreatus. *Biochem. Biophys. Res. Commun.* 275:810-816.

Wick, W., Grimmel, C., Wagenknecht, B., Dichgans, J. and M. Weller. 1999. Betulinic acid-induced apoptosis in glioma cells: A sequential requirement for new protein synthesis, formation of reaction oxygen species, and caspase processing. *J. Pharmacol. Exp. Ther.* 289:1306-1312.

Willmann, M. et al. 2009. Characterization of NVX-207, a novel betulinic acid-derived anti-cancer compound. *Eur. J. Clin. Invest.* 39:384.

Winther, K., Apel, K. and G. Thamsborg. 2005. A powder made from seeds and shells of a rose-hip subspecies (*Rosa canina*) reduces symptoms of knew and hip osteoarhritis: A randomized, double-blind placebo controlled trial. *Scand J. Rheumatol.* 34:302.

Yesilada, E., et al. 1997. Inhibitory effects of Turkish folk remedies on inflammatory cytokin: interleukin-1 alpha, interleukin-1 beta, and tumor necrosis factor alpha. *J. Ethnopharmacol.* 58:59-73.

Ying-Mee, T., Yu, Rong, and J. M. Pezzuto. 2003. Betulinic acid-induced programmed cell death in human melanoma cells involves mitogen-activated protein kinase activation. *Clinical Cancer Research.* 9:2866.

Index

S-T

U-Z

32 topically
151 infusion 201
165 oil of fennel, parasites
205 vegans
214 Menial
150 Alcohol tinctures